PRAISE AND UNSOLICITED COMMENTARY
(from authors, suitors and other very important people)

"Sandi Amorello's *The Irreverent Widow* is a laugh-till-you-cry, cry-till-you-laugh memoir that offers advice on grieving, single parenting, dating, and sex after 40, not to mention etiquette and a whole lot of wisdom on life. Sandi's hilarious and unapologetic truth-telling is inspiring and instructive. Most certainly *not* for widows only."

—Jane Pollak, author, *Soul Proprietor:*
101 Lessons from a Lifestyle Entrepreneur

"You are too funny. OK, yes I am extremely handsome and very fit. I love to work out. I might describe myself as looking like the actor Ben Affleck, but probably better looking."

—PerfectOne, Match.com, 2004

"Sandi Amorello's book is not just for those readers who have lost a spouse but for anyone who has ever wholly loved another person, flaws and all, and recognized that with the roses there are bound to be thorns…not to mention weeds, bees, aphids, and blackspot. She writes about genuine sorrows, while never losing sight of the interwoven surprises of joy, in a forthright, sometimes flirtatious prose that avoids sentimentality and offers—despite her subject—considerable space for laughter. Granted, the humor can be edged. I love her take on Kubler-Ross, for example, the approximately 93 stages of grief: 'Shock. Denial. Swearing. Denial. Crying. Crying. Crying. Anger. More swearing. Panic. Denial. Desperation. Denial. Crying. Crying. Crying. A lot more swearing. More anger. Envy. Crying. Crying. Crying…' Amorello doesn't sugarcoat the grief, nor offer any platitudes on how to heal; she simply tells us her story, and that is enough in itself."

—Ann E. Michael, author, *Water-Rites*

"I am certain the book you eventually write will make the best-seller list—so I will need a signed copy when it comes out."

—C., Match.com, 2004

"I have not kissed like that since 1988 (truthfully). "

—K., Match.com, 2003

"This is the kind of book that you wish you had when you were in college, full of things you wish your wise, worldly best friend had told you before you started dating in earnest. *The Irreverent Widow* is not just for the widowed but for all who are dating (men included—in fact, men in particular), and maybe even those who aren't. Sandi covers the universal themes of forgiveness, consideration (and quite a lot of the lack thereof: who gives a bereaved family four slices—less than half—of a $2.50 jelly roll along with potato-chip-encrusted chicken leftovers as part of their we're-trying-to-help-you-by-making-dinner-for-you-while-you're-mourning dinner?), and love, from the perspective of someone who has known real love and is confident enough in herself to share self-deprecating, sometimes downright embarrassing stories that will cause you to alternate between sobbing and erupting in actual out-loud, spit-your-drink-out laughter. Share this book with all of your friends. All of them. They'll thank you for it."

—Amy McCoy, author, *The Poor Girl Gourmet*

"I am a happy combination of naughty and nice. You should be, too. If you are not at all nice, you may earn a paragraph in the book I will be penning one day soon. Exhibit *really* bad behavior, and you may earn your very own chapter."

—Sandi Amorello, 2007

"Whoever you are, you write very well. Sadly, I'm too old, too short, and too far away. Plus my subscription expires in a few hours. Oh well, it was still a great read…."

—Match.com guy in Pennsylvania, 2005

"I think I would like to drink Merlot with you on the beach. After that, I would like to give you a back rub. Can you please send a picture?"

—LookingForYou, Match.com, 2004

"The notion that 'life goes on' after a devastating loss—particularly the loss of a young spouse and the co-parent of one's children—can be exceedingly difficult for the spouse left behind. But Sandi Amorello's *The Irreverent Widow* proves that life not only goes on, it can once again be joyful and rich with promise. With humor, irreverence, and an unquenchable life force, Sandi Amorello shares the truths she learns about grief, single parenting, and allowing love back in her life. *The Irreverent Widow* is an honest and upbeat story that will reassure anyone who grieves, or has ever grieved, that healing and happiness do lie ahead."

—Jessica Bram, author, *Happily Ever After Divorce: Notes of a Joyful Journey*

"I think when you finally get your screenplay together you could well have something to trot in front of Christopher Guest."

—BoatGuy, Match.com, 2003

"You're going to get the ellipses overuse award for 2012. Yikes."

—Alan Rinzler, editor extraordinaire, 2012

"Wow, Mom! I'm so proud of you! So…are we making any money yet?"

—Holden Amorello, skeptic, 2008

The Irreverent Widow

Shockingly true tales of love, death
and dating...with children in tow

Sandi Amorello

The Irreverent Widow

Shockingly true tales of love, death and dating…with children in tow

Published by Silver Crayon Studios

Library of Congress control # 2012917108
The Irreverent Widow / Sandi Amorello

ISBN 978-0-9859874-0-4

Printed in the United States of America

Cover design and layout: Cooley Design Lab
Cover graphic: Nick Hall
Author photograph: Kevin Brusie

DEDICATION

For the man whose smile
will forever live in my heart, and light my way.

I know you're laughing, sweetie
…wherever you are.

Thank you for loving me.

ACKNOWLEDGMENTS

My mother always taught me to say thank you. That said, I would still feel compelled, even if she hadn't raised me so well.

Much gratitude to Alan Rinzler, editor extraordinaire. An exceedingly patient, talented and generous man who made me write, rewrite, rewrite again...and smile all along the way (and who also cured me of my ellipses addiction without the need of a rehab facility). Thanks also to Leslie Tilley, my copy editor, who kindly took me on and taught me, once again, that editors are wondrous creatures who do magical things with words that leave me in awe.

Thanks to Steve Cooley, for succumbing to my endless emails and offering up his design talents. And for being so excited about this project that he managed to fit me into his uber-busy schedule.

An abundance of love and thanks to my mother, Louise, for supporting my creativity, always, and never questioning my determination to go to an art college. Had she been more practical, and forced me to become a biologist (my backup career choice), I'd be writing about microscopic life forms and would never had met Drew, or given birth to our three children.

Speaking of whom...Olivia, Holden, and Cole, there aren't words to describe how much I love and cherish you. Your dad would be so proud of you. And the best part is, I know that you know that. You were my reason for waking up when he first died, and my reason to keep going when I didn't think I could go any further. I love you more than I could have ever imagined when I was in the throes of labor (especially labor with the one in possession of the gigantic noggin—you know who you are!).

Thank you, Doug, for being such an expressive and caring brother, to the Amorello family for their love and support, and to my wonderful friends, old and new, near and far, who have been a source of strength, laughter, and have been there to listen to me whine when I didn't want to keep reading my own writing. My heartfelt thanks to Jane and Darcey for helping to push me up the mountain, to the Robinson brothers for believing in me and treating me with kindness and patience, even when I was (quite possibly) on the verge of becoming an annoyance…and to Brian, for composing that email back in 2007 that so gently prodded me with the following sentiment: "So when are you going to write that f*cking book?!"

Lastly, thank you to all of the men I've dated since being thrown into the wild world of widowhood—without you, chapters 7, 9, and 12 wouldn't be possible.

*Names and other identifying tidbits have been changed
to protect the innocent…and not so innocent.*

CONTENTS

INTRODUCTION

*If I had no sense of humor, I would have long ago
committed suicide.* —Mahatma Gandhi

I love Gandhi. Were he alive today, I'd go out for a latte with him
in a heartbeat. He obviously knew the value of laughter in the
face of tragedy, and I'll bet he was more fun to be with than 85
percent of the men I've dated since my husband died.

Welcome, dear reader, to the world of widowhood. If you're
feeling brave, I invite you to take a glimpse into the made-for-
TV-movie that is sometimes my life. I warn you up front, this
is not for the faint of heart. You may find yourself crying until
you laugh and laughing until you cry. Which is basically how
I've managed to retain my sanity since becoming what I call an
Irreverent Widow.

My name is Sandi Amorello. I live in an idyllic town on the
coast of Maine with my three witty, wonderful children: Olivia,
Holden, and Cole, ages nineteen, sixteen, and thirteen. We
moved here from just outside of Boston in 2005, with two cats,
one fish, and a dwarf hamster in tow.

In the happily-ever-after fairy tale version of my life, I was
married to my loving, sensitive, silly, charming, funny, and
handsome college sweetheart, Drew. Unfortunately, he left us
nine years, one state, three pet rodents, and two houses ago.

Diagnosed with terminal cancer shortly after his 40th birthday
as the daffodils were peeking up through the soil of our garden

in the early spring of 2000, he died two-and-a-half years later, as the Christmas snow sparkled in our pine trees on the 26th of December 2002. His funeral was on New Year's Eve, and I woke up on the first day of that year wishing I were lying beside him in a doublewide coffin. It was the innocent faces of my children, then four, seven and nine, combined with unfounded optimism and an inborn sense of humor, that kept me from dying of a broken heart.

At the time, I didn't consider myself particularly young at forty-one, although looking back at the photographic evidence, I was. We all were. All five of us.

Being widowed is not fun. It has, however, turned out to be rather funny at times. In between the tears, that is. One day you're going along, trying to survive the day-to-day challenges of raising three little children with a man you've loved forever. A man with whom you happily share a house, a bathroom, and a bed. The next day you're logged onto Match.com at one a.m., getting emails from men who want to drink merlot on the beach with you and give you a back rub. Men with screen names like The Gregster and BetrayedAgain. Men who are not your husband. Men who might have restraining orders against them. Dear God.

As you may already know, life doesn't always go quite as we plan.

I never intended to go on this journey, and never in my wildest imagination or worst nightmares could I have foreseen this tragic turn of events. However, now that I'm here, I have to admit, there is a silver lining.

Just to be clear, I didn't come home from the funeral, put on a party dress, and head out for a night on the town. I miss my husband immensely. I continue to miss him every day, for myself and, more than anything, for my children. That said, I have something many women never get—an opportunity to reinvent myself, and to be with a completely different sort of man if I wish to be. And I had a wonderful, perfectly imperfect first marriage. How many women get to have a fairytale romance, and then have a chance to experience a completely different storyline?

It's not that I wouldn't give anything to have my adoring husband back, it's just that I choose to see the gift in having been given the chance at a second life, all within the same lifetime. My other option is to climb back under the covers and cry, so I figure I'd best put my energy into making the best of "Plan B."

When I fell in love and got married, I never thought the "till death do you part" thing would actually happen when I was only forty-one. I thought maybe somewhere around age ninety-two we'd die simultaneously in a plane crash, or from drinking a few too many martinis while we were on heart medication. It never occurred to me that fourteen years and three kids later, he'd check out on me. Never.

I mean, who ever thinks of that sort of thing?

We go through the day-to-day moments of our lives often oblivious to the perfection of our existence. Then, the unthinkable happens; the world turns upside-down, and our reality changes in an instant. It's one of those things we always think happens to "someone else," and then suddenly, we are the ones trapped inside the bubble, looking out.

Having been trained as an illustrator, I find it wonderfully gratifying and amusing that I am also now a storyteller, sharing my stories via my art *and* my writing. (My mother is finally seeing her tuition dollars put to work, and she is thrilled.)

My stories contain a lot of humor. For me, a sense of humor and creativity is what has saved me from nine years of antidepressants, potential alcoholism, and child abandonment. It's who I am, how I express myself, and how I get through life. It's enabled me to climb out of the depths of hell and heal my heart.

Some people find this unsettling, because although it's obviously easy to find humor in things like dating and single-parenting—two arenas where ridiculousness is just a given—tragedy is another thing altogether. But I'm merely doing what has always come naturally to me…finding humor in the seemingly humorless. Making sense of the disappointments and heartaches of life by looking for that one little kernel of good. That one little ray of sunshine. That one little obscenity that holds within it the potential to make a beverage come shooting out of your nose.

So I've gathered some of these stories, journal entries, columns, and blog posts that I've penned since attaining my highly undesirable and not at all glamorous widowed status and turned them into this first book of mine. And I've done it for me and for you. Because if we're not here to help one another, then what's it all about, really?

I'm not going to get all preachy, or tell you that a religious figure appeared to me in a dream with the secret to "speed-grieving." I'm merely here to share with you my own quirky stories: tales of loss, love, lust, death, devastation, desperation, frustration, tears, romance, adventure, laughter, heartache, probable insanity… and a few fleeting moments of what appear to be some brand of possible enlightenment.

I am here to share with you truths about grief, single-parenting, and midlife courtship that most women would never share. Or admit. I'll tell you things that would make your therapist shake her head in shock and dismay. But, hey, did your therapist walk behind her husband's casket, flanked by her three young children recently?

The bad part is that my wonderful husband is dead. The good part is that I was married to a man who adored and loved me completely, and so, now that I'm dating again, I have standards that are quite high. I know what it's like to be in a wonderful relationship and marriage, and I won't settle for less the second time around, if I indeed even decide that I want a second time around. Which is a huge *if.*

In the beginning, I sat around crying for hours, days, weeks, and months. All right, years. I cried for years. I still cry. I will most likely always cry for what I have lost.

I read the books, went to the support groups, and I didn't get much out of any of it. I just wanted someone to give me hope that I'd smile again, have a life again, and maybe even have great sex again. Someone to tell me that it was OK (and maybe even normal) to entertain thoughts of selling my three children and ending my own life to be with my husband who was six feet under the ground—as long as I didn't actually do it. Someone to be honest and tell me it was OK to hate him and love him and curse him for not keeping his promise to be with me forever.

I longed for lighthearted, hard-earned wisdom and inspiration. Now that I have made it this far, and no longer own stock in the company that makes Kleenex, I am hoping I can inspire someone else, to assure you that you're not the only one who might be lying in bed alone at night, reading cheesy self-help books, thinking, *There must be someone who understands—and isn't so damned depressing!*

Nearly ten years later, the tears have stopped flowing on a daily basis, and Drew is tucked safely in a corner of my heart. I still love him, but have room now for someone else. I follow my heart and my dreams, and I wake up each morning, thankful that my children and I are still laughing.

I know that would please Drew more than anyone, and I hope it makes you smile, too.

PART ONE: Shock and Grief

1

DEATH

We were two months into the much-anticipated and much-hyped "new millennium," and my husband, Drew, was about to turn forty. Coincidentally, it was just around the time of this momentous birthday that his skin suddenly took on an unsettling, yellowish glow. Since he was a normally healthy guy, we all, including his doctor, assumed that something was amiss with his gall bladder. No big deal; a test or two, a minimally invasive surgical procedure, in and out of the local hospital in half a day, and he'd be down on the floor with the kids, knee deep in Legos and Play-Doh once again.

As a woman who had given birth to three quite sizeable children, mostly without the use of pain medications, to me having a gall bladder sucked out of one's body seemed like nothing to write home about.

Living just outside of Boston meant that competent doctors and five-star hospitals were plentiful. So Drew went in for tests, and then more tests. Followed by more tests. And suddenly, it became clear that everything they thought it might be—well, it wasn't. I realized then that a medical diagnosis is often a hit-or-miss process of elimination conducted in the dark, as opposed to a home run hit over the center field wall under the bright lights at Fenway Park. What we didn't count on was the tests coming back inconclusive. What we didn't count on, ultimately, was pancreatic cancer.

With every test, and every torturous waiting-for-results smattering of days, the seedlings of fear inside of my stomach, heart, and head grew stronger. I tried to remain positive, I tried not to allow my true feelings to show in front of Drew and, especially, the children. I tried to believe well-meaning neighbors, friends, and family members who would hug me as tears welled up in my eyes, to reassure me that all would be well.

But all wasn't well. And finally, after there were no other conclusions to be reached, the head of surgery at a certain top-notch Boston hospital looked us in the eyes and told us he was approximately 97 percent sure that when they operated, they would find a tumor on Drew's pancreas. A malignant one.

Surgery—scheduled for April 28th—was something called the Whipple procedure. A doctor sat us down a couple of weeks before the big day and, on a piece of paper with a black outline of a human body, drew what appeared to be random red slash marks indicating all the things that would be subsequently removed from my husband's digestive system.

We observed in near silence, shook the surgeon's hand, walked out to the parking garage, climbed into our red Ford Explorer, and proceeded to cry in one another's arms until there were no more tears left to fall.

The date of his surgery remains burned into my brain: it was my only sibling Doug's thirty-third birthday. We didn't find out until afterwards that the Whipple procedure was, apparently, one short step down the scale from open-heart surgery. I sat in a room filled with other anxious people for over six hours, as the clock ticked and the sun fell lower in the sky. Finally, the surgeon came up to tell me the news. It was everything I didn't want to hear.

Being a healthy forty-year-old man (if you don't count the terminal cancer), Drew recovered amazingly quickly from the surgery itself—which was really not a last-ditch effort but an "only-ditch" effort, used to slow down the cancer process by removing the tumor itself and goodly amounts of surrounding internal organs. With pancreatic cancer, as with other cancers with a very poor prognosis, the problem lies in the fact that by the time symptoms appear those sneaky cells have usually quietly infiltrated your body. With no early warning system, you're left with not much more than a wing and a prayer. And, if you're very fortunate, a gifted surgeon who can buy you time, so that you can be there to blow out the candles on a few more of your children's birthday cakes.

Drew was back home in a week and back at work in two. His spirit and inner strength were truly inspiring—not just to me, but to the world around us.

PALLIATIVE IS A FOUR-LETTER WORD

Palliative is a word you don't want to hear when you are being spoken to about cancer treatment options. As it turned out, other than surgery, there was no real treatment for pancreatic cancer. The survival rate at that time was less than 1 percent. I don't think it's much improved since then, either. Still, Drew felt as if anything they were offering was better than doing nothing, and so he endured three months of chemotherapy "treatments," in conjunction with radiation. The chemo drug was dubbed 5-FU, which, as you might imagine, we found extraordinarily appropriate. It was responsible for our first glimpse into "cancer humor."

One morning, in the weeks after he had first turned the color of pale mustard but before anyone had breathed the word *cancer,* I lay in our bed and looked out our window at the shadows of the tender green leaves on the oak trees and the color of the house across the way, where we had once lived. I felt as if I were trapped inside someone else's body. I remember my stomach clenching, my nerve endings tingling with a sense of dread, and the tears coming to my eyes. I held them back because he was in bed, beside me, and I didn't want him to know I was afraid.

It was the first time I truly understood what it meant to be trapped in a nightmare. During the years we had been together, Drew would sometimes be fast asleep next to me, only to suddenly erupt into a state of noisy panic. I'd have to physically shake him to awaken him from his bad dream, and he'd always tell me later that he had wanted to move, to open up his eyes, but he couldn't. He was trapped.

Now I completely understood how he had felt.

So it all started with the dawn of the new millennium. And it all ended precisely three holiday seasons later.

DECK THE HALLS

The spirit of Christmas is not easily frightened off. Not even by white lab coats and oxygen tanks. As in Dr. Seuss's beloved *How the Grinch Stole Christmas*, it doesn't come from a box. It comes from the heart. And, whether you want it to or not, it will even follow you into the hospital.

Through the revolving door…up the elevator…down the long, lonely corridors with the cold, fluorescent lighting, it follows. Though it doesn't feel right that it should be there, in a place filled with the scent of disinfectants and bad food, instead of balsam and gingerbread.

Any Christmas entangled with illness is difficult, but the holiday season that had Drew lying in the hospital, dying, was unbearable. And it wasn't the presence of the spirit of Christmas that bothered me that December, so much as the presence of wreaths and little elves purchased at church fairs and jingle bells hanging from hospital doorknobs. It was sad. It was depressing. It was just wrong. To me, anyway.

Now maybe some people would still be cheered by the whole message of Christmas. Maybe the tacky decorations would be a reminder of that message, providing some sort of strangely comforting, uplifting feeling. For me it was just the opposite. It did not comfort me. It did not uplift me. It sickened me and saddened me and made me want to toss our vintage family crèche into the fireplace, along with the Yule log.

Our middle child was in the first grade when his father was in the hospital, battling those final weeks of cancer. His classmates made a chain.

A bright, colorful, happy chain out of construction paper. Full of individual Christmas wishes. "Merry Christmas, Mr. Amorello"… "We hope you feel better soon, Mr. Amorello"…"We love you, Holden's Dad." Wishes of hope and holiday spirit, announced in crayon across carefully cut strips of colored paper from an educational art supply store. Happy, lovely, heartfelt thoughts that could only be written by six-year-olds. Children who didn't know what cancer was. Children who didn't know that, as they prepared for another happy Christmas with their daddies, their classmate was preparing for the final Christmas with his.

I would save that paper chain of well wishes that we hung from Drew's singular hospital window for years. Finally, though, I had to throw it away. I could no longer tolerate the pain it evoked each time I stumbled upon it. The lump of construction paper sentiment stuck in my throat and seemed to want to choke me. Only a child could hang that above his father's deathbed. Only a child could do that, without tears.

One of my favorite quotes says, "It is good to be children sometimes and never better than at Christmas." I'm here to tell you, that is true.

Thank goodness for children.

THE END

Amazingly, Drew had remained symptom-free and we lived a kind-of-normal life until August of 2002. Which is when we found out about the recurrence.

We had promised to take the children to Disney World in November, so we moved that up to September, instead. By Thanksgiving, things were not good. By Christmastime, he was in the hospital and things were more than not good.

Drew came home on Christmas Eve. A twilight ambulance ride that I shall never forget in this lifetime or the next. We arrived to find our beautiful little Beatrix Potter house in the woods decorated and glowing with magical, tiny white lights. The EMTs made tracks through the snow as they carried him into the house on a stretcher. Past the Christmas tree, past the train set that he never got to see, past our children. And up the stairs to our bedroom for the last time.

I wish I could tell you that the next thirty-nine hours were a blur, but they remain crystal clear. I sat on a dining room chair late on Christmas evening, my forehead pressed against the frozen glass of the multi-paned window of our beautiful little 1940s house. I can still feel that intense cold as it penetrated my soul. Like a dagger-shaped icicle slamming down atop my head...piercing my skull...piercing my brain. Making a direct path to my heart. I watched the snow fall through my tears, and I prayed that he would die. I sat there watching the most beautiful snow falling, on what would have otherwise been the picture of a perfect Christmas night, praying that the man I loved more than anyone in the world would die. My husband. My children's father.

I cried because I wanted his suffering to end. I cried more because I didn't want him to leave me. It was the most unselfish thing I have ever wished for in my life.

Drew died the next morning, December 26th. It was beautiful and sunny and the sparkling white snow hung thickly in the pine trees outside our second- floor bedroom window. A winter wonderland. A Christmas card. I smiled at him and told him to look at how beautiful it was outside, to look at the snow. He said he couldn't, that it hurt too much. I could see the tears in his eyes.

I wanted to think he just meant it was too bright outside, and that the sun hurt his eyes, but in my heart I knew him and I knew what he meant. It was too beautiful to look at, and it hurt too much, because he knew he was leaving it. The snow, the sun, this beautiful world that he loved so much…and us.

The next few minutes were an eternity. The family—our mothers, siblings, and a few of their spouses—gathered around his bed. Our children sat downstairs, playing with Christmas toys. I held his hand and kissed his face and thought how handsome he still was…even as he breathed his last breath.

His closest brother, who had been by Drew's side throughout all of this, arrived only moments later. The cry of despair that escaped his lips as he realized it was too late for a final good-bye still haunts me. A primeval groan that echoed from his soul, transcending time and language. I remember how it cut through me, like the cry of a wounded animal.

I took Drew's wedding ring off of his finger and walked down the flight of carpeted stairs, feeling as if I were floating in a state of timelessness, to tell our children the thing I never in my heart imagined I'd have to tell them—he was gone. And as I gathered the three of them on Olivia's bed, in a room decorated with flower fairies and glow-in-the-dark glitter and nine-year-old sunshine, I wondered how I was going to survive until the next moment.

THE FUTURE

When your husband is going to die, you don't believe it. Even when you hear the word *terminal*, you don't believe it. However, when your husband's heart has just stopped beating and his mother is standing in your kitchen with her slacks down around her knees because, along with being emotionally numb at the loss of her child, she has the as-yet-undiagnosed beginnings of Alzheimer's, and your four-year-old son is skipping cheerily through the house proclaiming in a sing-songy voice, "Daddy's dead! Daddy's dead!"…well, you begin to believe the nightmare you've just walked into.

You begin to believe your husband has left you. Forever.

There will be no custody battle. No expensive lawyers. No nasty letters or hurtful accusations. No arguments over who gets to keep the cappuccino machine or have the kids for the winter vacation. There will just be tears that spring forth from your soul. And your children's souls.

There will be casseroles and errant loaves of banana bread swathed in plastic wrap that appear on your front porch.

There will be heartache. And an eternal hollowness.

There will be darkness that will swallow you whole.

There will be no future. No hope. No consolation.

And you will wonder why. Why he was taken from you. Why they couldn't save him. Why your children have to grow up without him. Why you have to continue to wake up each day. Why most of your friends have a husband.

There will be a relentless ache in the center of your being unlike anything you have ever felt before. For yourself, and for your fatherless children.

Love will seem unfair and life will seem meaningless. Death will seem like a welcome option…

…Then, one day, you'll wake up and it will be seven years, six months, and nineteen days later…and you'll realize that you are in the middle of "the future."

And it's not quite so dark anymore. Your insides are filling up again.

Your children have somehow survived. Maybe even thrived.

And he is in their eyes and their smile and their laughter. He is in the way they stand on the Little League field with their hands in their pockets, and he is in the doodles on their sketchpad.

And you'll fall in love with him all over again. Tuck him back into that secret corner of your heart. Wake up each day and continue to breathe. Slowly and deeply. For yourself. For your children. And for him.

CRYING, CRYING…AND MORE CRYING

It wasn't bad enough that I spent forty-nine minutes out of every hour in tears. It wasn't bad enough that my eyes were so swollen that I could barely see. But, to add insult to injury, I also had tiny white bits of tissue lint all over everything. Stuck to my eyelashes. My nose. My cheeks. My chin. And those flecks of purity reminded me of the snow. Which reminded me of the wintry day Drew died, and of the snow at the cemetery, on the day of his funeral…which made me cry even more.

It was a vicious cycle that seemed to go on ad infinitum.

I still cry for what I've lost, and I most likely always will. Because no matter how much time has gone by, there is always a "trigger." Sometimes it's obvious: a holiday, a wedding, an anniversary. Or one of the children's special days: the first lost tooth, first Little League game, date, prom, college acceptance letter, graduation, boyfriend, girlfriend. Good Lord, the list is endless. It creates a highway of probable tears of sentiment that stretches as far into the future as you can see.

I have burst into tears at grocery stores, shoe stores, karate lessons, and school plays. I recall once retreating to the middle school faculty restroom for about twenty minutes in the middle of hanging up "memory posters" with the parents of other eighth graders in preparation for our children's upcoming celebration, because I couldn't stop weeping. Compiling a montage of your child's happy family photographs is not a fun assignment when her father has become a fading memory.

When you're in the midst of death, grief, tears, and weeping, wailing, and desperation, you often ask yourself, *Will it never end?*

In my experience, no, it won't. Not completely. It will, however, become much less intense, less consistent…and less painful. You won't believe it at first, but time will march forward, and your heart and your tear ducts will slowly recover.

Perhaps just in time for some other life crisis to kick in. Can you say *menopause*?

2
THE FUNERAL

THE DAY OF THE FUNERAL still remains crystal clear in my mind. Actually, what I have is a mental photo album of images from that day's events, and I have just strung them together and filed them under *Drew's Funeral*. It was the morning of New Year's Eve. I remember waking, dressing, peering into our bathroom mirror, and thinking I looked rather good for a woman who had been crying for approximately seven days straight. Maybe that's why I thought I looked pretty good. I couldn't see clearly.

I remember thinking that I absolutely had to look beautiful… for Drew.

I came downstairs, and my children were dressed in their special outfits, looking beautiful and handsome and sad. My brother took a photo of them, like the one you'd take before your daughter rushes out the door to the prom. It seemed so surreal and strange to me. Would my children one day want a photograph of themselves on the way to their father's funeral? I knew my brother meant well and he was grieving, too. Not thinking all that clearly, just like the rest of us.

The Episcopalian church, steeped in tradition, was made of stone. Gray stone. The temperature had risen that day, and there was an otherworldly fog rising from the frigid, snowy ground. Gray sky, stone, streets. Everything was a shade of gray—like the grayscale chart we'd had to meticulously paint during our freshman year at art college. The layer of soft, luminous gray had settled on everything, enshrouding us all.

In the church, I felt like I was in someone else's body. I sang every hymn, listened to every word of every passage read. Somehow, I was stronger than I ever imagined. It was kind of creepy, actually.

As they carried Drew's casket down the aisle of that church, I followed, carrying our four-year-old son, and leading our other two children by the hand. I'm not sure how I managed, considering I only had two arms, but I somehow did it. I could see the tears of those six or seven hundred people as they watched us. Their pain was almost palpable.

I didn't shed a tear. I was frozen inside.

And as we sat in the limousine on the long, winding country road that would lead us to the cemetery, I remained frozen. Clinging to the pieces of Drew that lived on in my children's little faces, to the light in their eyes…to their innocence. Their dependence on me for strength was what got me through that day, and many more to follow.

As we came around a curve in the road, there were horses up ahead, standing in the snow and the fog, draped in their flannel winter blankets. They were the same horses that we always passed on that section of the road out of town, only this time they were standing at the edge of their fence, looking at us. Quietly, peacefully, majestically. As if they were standing guard, paying tribute.

No one in the car spoke.

Drew had been a filmmaker, and this was a movie—beautiful, silent, black-and-white. One of Drew's good friends had said that Drew's life was like a movie, and now, his death was, too.

And this was an ending so captivating, he would have most certainly approved.

DRESSING FOR ETERNITY

Did you know that when your husband dies, not only do you have to find something for yourself to wear to the funeral, but you are also expected to choose clothing for him? I had no idea.

When the funeral home men showed up and asked me what I'd like him to wear, I thought they were joking. I don't know what I was thinking. It was a closed casket, and I guess I was thinking that Drew was going to leave this world naked, the same way he entered it. Or maybe in whatever it was he was wearing the morning he died. Something light green, perhaps, with letters stamped on it somewhere indicating the name of the hospital that would eventually want it back. I don't think he would have cared what he was wearing, to be honest. He was dead. But these funeral people cared, that's for sure. They took their work seriously.

There was no pressure, they said quite politely, but would I please find him some appropriate clothing, before they headed back to funeral home central? Funeral home people—what a depressing job. I know someone has to do it, and I am happy that ours were polite and well behaved, but still I found myself thinking, *I may be widowed, but at least I don't work in the funeral business.*

In the final analysis, it really was a no-brainer; Drew had to wear his favorite clothes, even if they couldn't zip up the jeans because of his altered state. Who would ever know, anyway? Did the great Creator care whether you showed up in a custom-made Italian fine wool suit and a $185 silk tie, or a 1980s polyester jogging ensemble and holes in your underwear? I think not. Of course, I would never dream of being buried in polyester, but there are people who would probably go that route. And, really, who cares at that point?

I stood in our bedroom, in front of his closet…and the image came to me as if through divine intervention. It was inspired funeral fashion.

I am happy to say that I remained true to who he really was and that my late, handsome husband is now traversing eternity outfitted in his favorite torn, faded (sexy) Levis, American flag-patterned Ralph Lauren boxer shorts, a white t-shirt with a dancing hula girl (whose breasts are tastefully covered by a hibiscus lei) emblazoned on the front, with a white, button-down, 100 percent cotton RL Polo oxford shirt over it…and bare feet.

I also had them slip into his back pocket the faded, crackly, laminated photo of the two of us from our college romance days that he always kept in his wallet. I know he can't take it out to look at it, but it just seemed appropriate that he take me along on his journey into eternity. You know, just in case we don't meet up later on…and it turns out death is more like a diving board than an endless interconnecting infinity symbol.

When I picture Drew in my mind now, I often see him in those clothes. Not the way he looked the last time I saw him, but the way I remember him looking in them as he was running out of the house to get us bagels and coffee on any given Saturday morning. Kissing me and the baby goodbye. A giggling toddler in one arm and a little seven-year-old girl trailing behind, asking, "Daddy, can I come along too?"

The answer was always yes.

THE CASKET

So, after twenty-four hours or so of consistent weeping, you go to the funeral home to make the necessary arrangements. Hopefully, someone has driven you there, because you are certainly in no condition to do the driving yourself. But you've got to get there somehow, because someone has to do it. Someone has to pick out the casket.

You are taken to a room to peruse samples of coffins. And not just coffins, but ornamentation to stick inside of or on top of the casket. Outlandish things like poly-resin replicas of base-balls and golf clubs and balls of yarn. Teddy bears. Shamrocks. I don't know. It is all rather laughable when you realize what a moneymaking scheme this whole "death" thing is. Not that you shouldn't purchase a nice casket for your loved one, but do we really need tacky accoutrements and bad decorating choices to accompany us into the afterlife?

I think not.

I was very pleased with my choice for Drew's final housing. A beautiful cherry casket; simple lines, nice grain. Tasteful. Sans ornamentation. He deserved nothing less.

THE FLOWERS

Picking out flowers is something you want to do when you are planning a wedding or a party. Not a funeral. And yet, there I was at the upscale, tasteful, artfully urban floral design place, debating the merits of an assortment of blossoms.

The entire flower-selection process made things even more tragic. There I sat, choosing many of the same flowers I had chosen fourteen years earlier for my wedding bouquet.

In the end, the flowers were lovely. Although the florist did screw up...they forgot our freesia. Our white, beautifully fragrant, graceful freesia.

It had been featured in my wedding bouquet, and Drew had worn a sprig of it in the buttonhole of his tux. It was the one truly meaningful thing I had ordered, and they knew it. And they botched it. Even in the midst of my grief—or perhaps because

I was in the midst of my grief—it annoyed the hell out of me.

Eventually, they offered an olive branch in the form of a gift certificate. Presumably so that I could order up a hundred dollars worth of white freesia on a day when I really wanted to wallow in self-pity. Being a flower with a good amount of longevity, it would fill my house with its sweet scent for a solid week or so, thereby providing me a minimum of seven days to be reminded not only of my wedding but of my groom's subsequent funeral as well.

Thanks, but no.

THE HEADSTONE

Being a widow trained in the visual arts, I had a bit of a different take on the entire headstone thing. It was not just a headstone—it was a design project.

I had an idea of what I wanted. But, more importantly, of what I didn't want. This is usually the basis of all great design...knowing what you hate.

Granted, many grief-stricken people do not care about the flora and font featured on their loved one's headstone. They just want to cross it off of their to-do list so they can get back to the business of crying and being miserable.

Not me. I saw this as a way to stand out from the masses. I wanted to express the creativity we had shared throughout our life together. And that is why it took me six times the normal amount of time to come up with the final design.

Drew was an artist and his creativity shown through in everything he touched. His career and his passion centered around filmmaking and all of the detail associated with the craft. But his second passion was giving new life to things from the past. Things that had been neglected…things that needed someone with the love and patience required to bring out their beauty. He loved old stuff and would restore anything he could get his hands on: an old bureau left on the side of the road, a milking stool from a farm in Vermont, a house that needed tender, loving care to shine brightly once again. He appreciated the beauty of wood grain or the intricate design of a door's finely crafted metal lock plate just as much as the way antique glass rippled in the sunlight.

Drew especially appreciated work that was done the old- fashioned way…painstakingly, and by hand. I was most certainly not going to have some newfangled laser-cutter used to carve the stone that would mark his eternal resting place. I had this romantic image in my mind of a little old man with an Italian accent, suspenders, and a wool snap-brim cap, chiseling away, hour after hour, making the design I had drawn out on paper materialize in a beautiful piece of gray, unpolished granite.

The headstone ended up being ready about a year after Drew's death, and it was worth the time and effort. The only headstone in that cemetery featuring a whimsical, vintage angel with stars and a moon floating above and around its head, it looks as though it could be the headstone on the grave of a child. And although Drew was 42 when he died, we did have children, and he always held onto the child still inside of him. I know he would love it. It's a bit magical and mystical...not at all serious or stuffy. The last thing I wanted was for the man I love to spend eternity with a forlorn Jesus on a cross perched on top of him.

As they say, it's not final till it's carved in stone. And, thousands of chisel strokes later...it is. By hand.

3
LIFE AFTER DEATH

WHEN YOUR HUSBAND has been cheating death for a good long time after a terminal illness diagnosis, you almost begin to forget that one day the funeral may indeed really arrive. You remain hopeful and optimistic, certain that he is part of that amazingly fortunate "less than 1 percent" survival statistic. You can't see yourself living without him, and you can't allow yourself to look forward in time...to that imagined hollow moment following the one when his heart stops beating.

You don't see tomorrow, because you don't want to. And, there's no need to until, of course, tomorrow arrives.

After the proper authorities had been notified, and the death certificate had been issued, and the funeral home men had arrived to place the man I loved in a body bag and carry him down the flight of stairs from the warmth of our bedroom to the chill of the hearse, there was a stifling stillness. And I found myself filled with an urgent and desperate need to fill it.

Eventually, the tears stopped for a bit and the numbness kicked in. Like a wartime sergeant, seasoned in battle, I took charge and enlisted family members to do what I felt must be done: remove all traces of the hospital-y stuff that had filled our bedroom. The rented bed, the IV equipment, the bags and boxes of now never-to-be-used experimental medications we had once dreamt might save him.

The house quietly swarmed with people barely able to move. Like bumble bees in wintertime. The air I inhaled felt thick with death. My own mom and brother were there, along with Drew's mother, a goodly portion of his eight siblings and their spouses, and, of course, our three children.

Many of Drew's family members were still in that sleepy morning-after-Christmas mode, having had some brand of celebration the day before. (Just because our holiday had been less than joyful didn't mean their little families needed to suffer, too.) Though it's nearly unfathomable while in the midst of death, life does go on for those around us. Even when they share the same DNA.

My memories of our children during the days between the death and the funeral are scattered and blurry. I was in a widow's coma, induced by both my own disabling grief and the jolting pain of my children's new reality. They would forever after identify themselves as someone whose father "died when I was nine." Or seven. Or four. The magical childhood and adoring father I thought I had secured for them, the childhood that was supposed to make up for my own imperfect childhood and distant father, had disappeared with Drew's last breath. And I could barely allow that new reality to seep in.

I remember endless hugs and kisses and tears that welled up from the depths of their little souls. And I remember feeling as if I wanted to scream but someone was choking me, so all that came out was silence. I remember holding onto them for dear life, praying that their innocence and energy could sustain me as I dealt with the arrangements for their daddy's funeral.

My mother, Louise, had been a pillar of strength during the entire two years and nine months of our pancreatic cancer journey, from diagnosis to death. With a combination of tenderness, love, optimism, and wonderful cooking skills, she somehow mothered all of us—our children, myself, and Drew—even while his own widowed mother was losing her mental capabilities.

My mom's hard work and dedication had allowed me to be there for Drew in every possible way, especially during the final stages of his illness. And for this extraordinary gift, I will be forever grateful. She earned the title our then-minister had bestowed upon her, "Saint Louise," many times over.

Drew and Louise had always had a special relationship, and he had always been like a biological son to her. And you know that saying, the one about women marrying their fathers? Well, I always joked that instead of marrying "my father," an emotionally detached man with whom I'd had no relationship since my college days, I had been wise (or just lucky) enough to have married my mother. A much healthier choice in my case, trust me.

I'm pretty certain this quirky fact is part of what contributed to my long and happy relationship with my husband. My own estranged father had died of cancer long before Drew did. We didn't attend his funeral, and I'm rather certain had he still been alive, he wouldn't have attended Drew's, either. Drew's own father had passed away from stomach cancer the year before we were married, leaving his mother heartbroken and lonely after nearly four decades of marriage.

I never understood my mother-in-law's pain until her son died as I held his hand. Then suddenly, I loved her in a way I never could have in the past. Sadly, she was on the precipice of a plunge into the depths of Alzheimer's. In the years since her own death, I've imagined it was a blessing to her to no longer remember the pain of her many losses.

HIS BIRTHDAY

Journal entry

My love,

Today is March 6th, your birthday. It is ten weeks since the day you left. We had a snowstorm today and it was beautiful…big fluffy, white clumps falling from the sky. I went out and met our friend Sylvia for lunch. A treacherous, lovely drive.

I didn't care about the treachery; I needed to get out of here for a bit, away from this house where you died. To feel the cold air on my face and the snowflakes melting on my skin.

The florist delivered a gorgeous bouquet of white freesia, to make up for their funeral faux pas, and the scent is luscious. I didn't think I'd want to remember our wedding flowers, but I do. I brought them upstairs so I can smell them while I sleep tonight. I hope I will dream of you. I don't dream of you often enough.

Last night I remembered part of a dream I had about you and Chris. You were laughing and joking around, and had been out till three in the morning having so much fun. When I asked you what was so funny, you both just told me I wouldn't understand what you were laughing about. It made me happy, to remember how close you always were as brothers, and how much happiness you had shared in your lifetime.

Tonight I took the children out to celebrate (if that's what you would call it) your 43rd birthday. Without you. We went to Naked Fish, and it was actually quite nice. Not too many tears. They were very well behaved, and even ate their food. I had a yummy dinner—your favorite and mine—the roasted Chilean sea bass and some black bean soup and a house salad. Yum. And a glass of wine to toast your life. The kids and I all clinked glasses and said *Prosit* and I wished you a happy birthday. By the way, at lunch, Sylvia and I had huge, juicy burgers with fries and pickles in your honor. No soy burgers for me today. Screw that.

I went to the cemetery around five o'clock, in the middle of the snowstorm, because I just had to, that's all. I brought along a few stems of the freesia, but I couldn't really find your grave with the mountains of snow on top, although I think I got close. We've had so much snow this winter—you would have loved it.

There is so much I miss about you. Just those everyday little things…you walking through the door or calling me unexpectedly just to say hi. The smell of your cologne, the warm brown color of your eyes, the way you lit up the room when you smiled. But most of all, I miss your arms around me, and your soft, delicious kisses that made me melt into you.

Remember our song: "I'll Stop the World and Melt with You"?

Well, I wish I could stop the world right now. I hardly want to be here anymore. I love you. I will see you my love.

My heart is yours always,

Sandi

YOUR BIRTHDAY

What do you do on your birthday when your husband has just died?

Cry about the fact that he is no longer here to bake (or buy) you a cake, and won't be one of the faces at the table, singing the "Happy Birthday to You" song, and giving you a kiss laced with chocolate frosting later on…after the kids go to bed.

Buy yourself a really, really nice birthday present.

Buy yourself another one.

Because that's all you have at this moment, to fill the gaping hole in your heart.

YOUR CHILDREN'S BIRTHDAYS

Curse him for leaving you here to plan and carry out birthday parties for all three children every year from here on in. Be especially annoyed at him for having been so wonderfully creative in his orchestration and design of the three children's birthday parties every year, while he was alive. Curse him for your six-year-old's last birthday party, when he made the papier-mâché dinosaur eggs, and filled them with goodies…and then hid them outside in the freezing cold December weather, so the little kids could hunt for them. Curse him for forgetting to fill the eggs before letting the papier-mâché harden—and for making you laugh when he finally had to saw through each hard, glossy, beautifully crafted, professional quality egg to put the goodies inside.

Do your best. Buy a cake. Invite some kids. Try not to cry when they sing happy birthday and he's not there to take the photos with his vintage 1920s square- format camera that only uses black-and-white film from the special photo place.

Buy your child a really, really nice birthday present.

Buy yourself a really, really nice present too, while you're at it.

Buy yourself another one.

4
PULLING MYSELF TOGETHER

IF YOU ARE FORTUNATE, your spouse was not a pack rat. Mine was. (Forgive me sweetie, but I cannot tell a lie.) He was a selective pack rat, but a pack rat nonetheless. So, after all of the visitors stopped visiting and after the loaves of banana bread stopped mysteriously appearing on our doorstep, I realized I had an awful lot of cleaning out to do.

I started peeking into his closets, his bureau drawers, his boxes in the attic—and the basement and the garage. It made me cry and it made me miss him. It also made me incredibly angry and pissed off. How dare he have left me with fourteen boxes of antique crap to sort through?! The stuff he was supposed to have sorted through years ago, the stuff he was supposed to have sold on eBay. And now, he went and died…and managed to get out of yet another project. It just wasn't fair.

His clothes

This is what you need to do.

Cry on his shirts, fondle his ties, bury your face in the lapels of his suits.

Try to catch a whiff of "him"...his warm, familiar scent. Go to sleep in his favorite flannel plaid shirt, the one with the frayed collar. Snuggle up in his fleece pullover. Hug his sweaters and cry a river of tears into them. Night after night. Day after day.

Then, save his favorite Burberry raincoat (the one that had belonged to his father) and his favorite cowboy boots. The ones he had on when you met him in college. Save them for your kids. Save his Stetson hat, too. Save a few faded, soft, cuddly things for yourself, so you have something of his to hug when it's your anniversary, or his birthday, and the emptiness is unbearable.

Then, call a local charitable organization and get rid of the rest of it. Really. Let go of it.

Note: If the church secretary is reading this...I never did get that receipt you said you would send me for my 2003 taxes. Thanks for staying on top of that in my hour of need. My accountant will be calling you shortly.

His stuff

If you are lucky and had a husband who was of a high moral fiber and made few mistakes, you will not find any unwelcome little "surprises" when emptying out the contents of his bureau drawers. You will not find love notes from a woman in Topeka, Kansas, hidden in a secret compartment, under his boxer shorts. You will not discover the key to a safe deposit box that you knew nothing about. You will not find out that he was a cross dresser who performed under the name Lola.

I was one of these fortunate women; I did not find any surprises of any sort.

I imagine some women are not quite so lucky. I cannot fathom anything worse than finding out your husband of thirty-five years was a bigamist with a gambling problem and a life insurance policy naming Heidi Floozy of Salt Lake City, Utah, as the beneficiary.

Death is bad enough without hidden surprises.

His junk

Get rid of it. All of it. That is all I have to say.

I DID OWN A VEHICLE…DIDN'T I?

Approximately two days after Drew died, I vaguely recall wanting to drive somewhere (probably to the pharmacy to get some more Visine), looking out at my driveway, and realizing that something was missing. That something being our vehicle.

In the midst of all the chaos and confusion and tears, I had, apparently, forgotten that I owned a red Ford Explorer…and that I had hitched a ride home in an ambulance with my husband on Christmas Eve, and left it in the hospital parking garage. I wondered how I could have forgotten that I owned a vehicle.

I wondered how I could have left it for over two days, not even realizing I had abandoned it. I wondered how much of a bill I was racking up at an exorbitant hourly rate.

I had always been amazed at the fact that you could be at a

hospital, dying of some horrible disease, say, perhaps, pancreatic cancer…paying them enormous sums of money for treatments that weren't even designed to cure, and yet they couldn't give you free parking. How could that be? They were charging you hundreds of dollars a day for your husband's hospital bed, but you still were expected to read the parking bill every night through your tears and cough up an additional $37.50. Unbelievable.

There's nothing like adding insult to injury, and sometimes you simply cannot process one more thing. Even a parking garage ticket.

PHOTOGRAPHS

Your husband dies, and you don't want to forget him. My worst fear (other than that I would never have sex again before I died) was that I would forget him. So, I surrounded myself with photographs of his handsome self. Photos in the living room, photos in the dining room, photos in the kitchen, den, bathroom, and laundry room.

This was comforting in the early days and weeks of widowhood. But as the months went by, it began to dawn on me that part of the reason I was crying every time I turned around was that, every time I turned around, I was looking at a photo of the man I loved instead of the actual, flesh-and-blood man.

I was tormenting myself.

I gradually began paring down the photographs, removing a couple here and there, little by little, until I was left with only a few in what I considered appropriate places.

I did, however, make one huge error in judgment. An error that could only be made by someone in the deep, dark trenches of grieving. I left a smiling photo of my handsome, dead husband on the night table next to his (now empty) side of the bed. This was OK, except that when I started dating someone from out of town about a year into my solitude, I left it there. The poor man. He would drive over two hours to see me, sneak in after my kids were fast asleep, and leave before they woke up. And in that short interim, he made love to me while Drew looked over his shoulder (or whatever body part was closest) from his place of honor on the bedside table.

Later on, after we were no longer dating but were, surprisingly, still friends, he told me that I might want to consider removing the photo. He imagined it would make it difficult, if not impossible, for even the most virile of men to perform at their best.

In all honesty, I had never even considered that as an issue. Looking back, of course, it's clear that I was out of my mind, stuck in my widowed, grief-filled fog, but desperately wanting to move on.

PLEASE STOP TRYING TO MAKE ME FEEL BETTER

... before I kill you

When her husband has just died, or is in the process of dying, please do not talk to your friend the widow (or soon to be widow) and compare the death or imminent death of her spouse to the death of your own mother, father, brother, sister, aunt, uncle, cousin, friend, dog, or goldfish.

In my lifetime, beginning at the age of nine, I have suffered a string of losses. I lost my grandmother, my closest cousin, my best friend, my grandfather, my father, my other grandfather, my grandmother, my future father-in-law, and assorted other relatives and acquaintances. I have also suffered through the deaths of an inordinate number of family pets.

And I am here to tell you, it is not the same.

Every death is a loss. Every death causes sadness and grief in different people to different degrees. But, the death of a spouse is much different, for one basic reason. When you lose your spouse, you lose your future. You lose the person who was supposed to spend the rest of your life with you. You lose the person who was supposed to share in raising your children and be there for you when your mother or father or grandmother or best friend dies.

When Drew died, I lost "our future." I had lost my lover, best friend, parenting partner...but most of all, my tomorrow.

INSUFFERABLE REMARKS

Example A: Christmas 2003, the Girl Scout mom

After hearing my response to her sensitively phrased inquiry as to how things were going this holiday season:

> *Oh, come on, you can't tell me this year isn't better than last year!*

Oh, that's right...last year my husband was actually dying at Christmas. This year, he's just dead. What was I thinking, telling you things were difficult?

Silly me.

Example B: Sometime in 2004, the divorcée

> *You're lucky to not have to deal with an ex-husband.*
> *I wish my husband were just dead.*

OK...I don't think I need to even comment on that.

Example C: August 2002, the local Episcopalian minister

This was said to Drew in reference to me, right after we found out about his recurrence. At the time Drew was still (a) very much alive and looking quite wonderful, and (b) very much not planning on being dead anytime soon.

> *So, do you think she is going to be OK after you're gone?*

I had left the room to go upstairs and check on the children when I overheard this question from the man of God, as he sat in my living room, looking quite healthy and happy. I ended up in my bedroom, in tears, and never did make it back down to say good-bye to him.

I hope he is reading this, and that he is never diagnosed with pancreatic cancer. And that perhaps he has found a profession better suited to his level of sensitivity.

Example D: November 2004, the Match. com date in the plaid flannel shirt

> *So, does your husband have your kids on the weekends?*

Now, let's see: you called me about thirteen times in an irritatingly aggressive effort to get a dinner date with me, yet now you seem to have forgotten that I am widowed…not divorced. Did you even really read my profile? I would say you are not getting a goodnight kiss—not that you would have anyway. In fact, I think I will just flirt with our cute waiter for the rest of this date, and then let you pay the bill.

Check please!

PLEASE STOP COOKING FOR US!

Chicken à la potato chips and other gastronomic tragedies

I'll start out here by saying that just because you are in mourning does not mean you have lost your taste buds. Incessant crying and extraordinary sadness may dampen your appetite, but not your ability to differentiate good food from bad.

When your husband dies, people want to be helpful. I don't want to sound ungrateful, although I most likely will, but I just need to say something. If you know a woman whose husband has died, and you would like to help out by providing food for her and her three young, grief-stricken children in the first few months of their loss…by all means, do it. But put some thought into it. I beg of you, if you're going to do it, put forth a bit of genuine effort.

In the months following Drew's death, my two oldest children were in the first and fourth grades. It was a lovely surprise when I got calls from both sets of "room mothers," informing me that each class had a plan to provide us with dinners once or twice a week for the next few months. I was overcome with emotion and gratitude, and I thought, *How lovely, how thoughtful...what a nice break for me. I won't have to cry* and *cook every single night.*

The fourth-grade class had parents dropping off home-cooked meals that were sometimes hard to recognize and, sadly, often ended up in the garbage disposal.

People generally meant well. They tried. Well, some of them tried. We got casseroles, casseroles, and more casseroles. In a blatant act of passive aggression, one mother brought us about eighteen pounds of American chop suey (a concoction usually consisting of some form of macaroni, hamburger and tomato sauce). This was after I had told her neither my children nor I really liked American chop suey. One woman brought us what were apparently the leftovers from a dinner she and her husband and three kids had eaten earlier that evening: A bag of frozen corn, some French fries, and a paper plate covered with foil that concealed strips of chicken coated in some sort of crushed-potato-chip mixture. And for dessert, a jellyroll from the local grocery store, packed full of yummy, artery-clogging, probably carcinogenic hydrogenated oil. So perhaps it's fortunate we were only given four slivers of the stuff, on another paper plate, with its own foil. (Evidently, the grief-stricken don't merit an entire $2.50 cake.)

The first-grade class, in contrast, decided to collect money from the parents of the children in the classroom and use that money to buy whatever takeout food we requested.

Some weeks, we'd ask for pizza...other weeks we'd ask for Chinese or Thai...and other weeks we'd get lasagna and salad from the little gourmet Italian deli in town. After months of palatable takeout food, there was actually still money left over (wow…those were generous parents!), and the class mother told me she'd use it to buy us a gift certificate to our favorite local restaurant so we could get yet more takeout over the summer.

To be fair, one night we did get a great homemade meal from the fourth-grade class. One parent actually owned a restaurant, and his wife made us some sort of stew and a strudel. Even though she had apparently forgotten to add the sugar to the strudel mixture, it was still quite wonderful. I mean, at least they really put forth some effort. If I recall, they even dropped off a bouquet of flowers with the meal.

No one ever brought me a bottle of wine though. An omission that left me very confused. If I ever know anyone who is widowed and trapped at home with three children, the first thing I would bring her would be a bottle of sauvignon blanc, a huge bunch of flowers, a chocolate fudge cake, and maybe a gift certificate for a massage, an offer to babysit…and a pizza for the kids. Leave the hydrogenated jellyrolls and frozen corn at home. Please.

P.S. I forgot to mention the twenty-seven loaves of banana bread.

PART TWO: Starting Over

5

FIRST STEPS–STUMBLING

THERE ARE MANY THEORIES about grieving, including a very popular one documented by the famous Swiss doctor, Elisabeth Kübler-Ross. I think it has a great deal of merit, and I am sure it has helped many people…but, when you're in the thick of it, reading about the process you will go through doesn't really help all that much.

I know they tell you there are five stages of grieving. I am here to tell you that although that is nice and tidy, my reality has involved about ninety-three stages, and I would categorize them a bit differently. For me, it has gone something like this:

> Shock. Denial. Swearing. Denial. Crying. Crying.
> Crying. Anger. More Swearing. Panic. Denial.
> Desperation. Denial. Crying. Crying. Crying. A lot
> more swearing. More anger. Envy. Crying. Crying.
> Crying. Anger. Anger. Anger. Swearing. Swearing.
> Swearing. Sobbing. Nausea. Sobbing. Despair. Despair.

Despair. Hopelessness. Depression. Envy. Hopelessness. Depression. Resentment. Resentment. Resentment. Envy. Despair. Crying. Crying. Crying. Depression. Anger. Rebellion. Hopelessness. Self-pity. Depression. Depression. Depression.

A general pissy, bad attitude.

More, more, more of the same.

And, finally…a glimmer of hope.

AUTONOMY

Yes, you can buy that crystal vase if you want to

A few short weeks into my widowhood, during the depths of a New England January, with darkness arriving at approximately five p.m. each night, I recall going out shopping while my mom was visiting.

It was a frigid evening and she offered to stay with the children as I headed to this huge warehouse-y kind of place where they had some beautiful brand-name clothing at discounted prices. They also had a small, decorative housewares section which I always enjoyed browsing through. I wasn't really looking to buy anything; as usual, I just needed to get out of my house.

I remember the moment I saw the vase—the vase that became a symbol of my newfound independence. It was thick-cut Swedish crystal and had polka dots etched into the surface. I thought it was a complete reflection of me. It was fine-quality, well-crafted, yet it had these dots etched into it that shouted, *I am a finely crafted, quality item, but I am also fun!*

I decided to buy it. I didn't have to wonder whether Drew would like it, I only had to worry about whether I liked it. It was a bittersweet moment. Realizing he wasn't going to be at home when I arrived with my purchase made me sad. But realizing that I could buy it without wondering if he was going to like it made me start to think—if I could buy a crystal vase with polka dots, it stood to reason that, if I was so inclined, I could also paint my living room orange.

I could do what I wanted to do without needing to compromise. I was suddenly flooded with a sense of liberation. It was an awakening. I was widowed, I was heartbroken, but maybe there were some teeny-tiny positives to this experience that I could focus on as time went by, when I could finally stop crying long enough to see them.

It was the first time I saw any sort of positive slant to any of this. And it gave me hope.

I put the vase into my shopping carriage. Then I grabbed a beautiful, long, black cashmere coat before heading over to the cashier. I doubt I really needed a coat. I did it, well, just because I realized I could. As I said, in the midst of my tears it was a glimmer of hope, and I was latching onto any tidbit of happiness that I could find.

No matter how small. Or materialistic.

FOLLOW YOUR BLISS

One of the worst things that happened after Drew died was that as the days and weeks and months dragged on, I realized that I no longer wanted to do any of the things that used to bring me joy. Art, antiquing—nothing appealed to me.

It was like suffering two deaths. The death of my husband and the death of the part of me that was passionate…and joyful.

I am an artist. Drew was an artist, too. We loved antiquing together—searching for silly, quirky things that we adored. We were both extremely creative. That was something that was woven into our everyday lives.

I can't describe the sadness that overcame me when I realized that I'd lost all of that, as well as Drew. I felt an ache inside of me that came from a deep, deep place. A place that belonged only to me. My creative, artistic spirit had been killed. It was gone, and the tears that flowed from my eyes came from a well so deep, there was nothing beyond it…not even an echo of hope. Because the thought of losing that part of me was like losing my own soul. Not just my soulmate, but my soul. I could not imagine how life would ever be worthwhile again if my own passions had been taken from me, along with my husband.

I suddenly and unexpectedly found myself grieving two losses.

Then one day, something miraculous happened. I woke up on a particular morning in June, about half a year after Drew's death, and I could literally smell the key to my future. I remember waking up, seeing the beautiful, early summer sunlight streaming into my bedroom…and smelling oil paints, and turpentine.

I could not get to the art supply store fast enough. I needed to start fresh and buy everything new—a new beginning. New paints, new brushes, and new turpentine.

I hadn't painted in oils since I was in college, and even then it wasn't a frequent occurrence. I had, however, spent most of my teenage years working in that medium. My very first painting, done at school in the fifth grade, was in oils. The painting caught the principal's eye and he asked me do another similar one for his office. Wow! Talk about an ego boost. Then my teacher mentioned to my mother that I had some apparent artistic inclinations, and, voilà, my art career had begun. For the next half dozen years, I took art lessons and spent much of those Saturdays painting with oil paints, exclusively.

They may have been messy and not particularly environmentally friendly, but they made me happy. Apparently, that feeling was still deep inside me waiting to be rediscovered.

That August we were invited to vacation at a friend's guesthouse on their idyllic farm in Vermont. My children rode off to camp on the minibus at 8:15 each weekday morning. Meanwhile, I spent eight hours each day, childfree and unfettered…drinking really good French roast coffee, eating pints of freshly picked raspberries from the local produce stand, hiking, reading, and listening to the birds sing. Best of all, I could paint. And paint. And paint.

I painted outside, each and every day. It was my heaven on earth.

The first day, I set up my easel on the back porch. I picked glorious white hydrangea from the front garden, arranged them in a vintage pottery vase purchased the day before at an antique store, and placed it on top of a wonderful cotton checkerboard blanket, which was also a recent vintage find.

I had the feeling it was once used as a beach blanket, or spread on the grass—home to a beautifully laid out picnic dinner, under the stars long, long ago. But that was probably just the romantic in me. I also plunked down some luxuriously ripe, downy-skinned apricots that I'd picked up at the local farm stand, as well.

I remember lifting my brush and, after that, lapsing into some sort of trance until midafternoon. I think I stopped once for a ten-minute food break, when I realized I had forgotten to eat all day. By the time I needed to reenter reality and pick up the children from camp, I had a finished painting.

I brought it into the house and propped it up against a wall, stood back, looked at it, and promptly burst into tears.

Looking at the painting I had just spent the morning and early afternoon working on, in that beautiful Vermont early-August light, I was completely overcome by a feeling of joy unlike anything I had experienced in a very long time.

I will never forget that feeling. It was one of renewal and rebirth, as if I had come alive again in a very important way. I had reclaimed a part of myself that I thought was lost forever—dead. But it wasn't! I wanted to not only cry, but dance and sing as well. In fact, I am sure I did just that. I also thanked God, the universe, and whomever else I thought deserved honorable mention, for giving me back that piece of myself. For giving me a sign. A sign that my life wasn't over. A sign that maybe it was just beginning. A different life from the one I had planned, but my life, nonetheless.

I looked at that painting, and the tears of joy rolling down my cheeks mixed with tears of sadness because I so wanted Drew to see it. I wanted him to smell the wonderful, warm, familiar art-college scent of those oil paints. But it wasn't his life anymore, it wasn't our life anymore…it was just mine.

And suddenly, it seemed imaginable that a life that was just mine could one day be enough. Maybe more than just enough.

FELIZ NAVIDAD

The first Christmas season that we faced alone also marked the one-year anniversary of his death. A double whammy. Any time of the year is a bad time to lose your husband…but Christmastime is a particularly bad time to die. Try to avoid it at all costs.

I pulled myself together. I avoided Christmas carols. I changed the radio station every time I'd hear the mere hint of a sleigh bell jingling during that first holiday season. But I couldn't cancel Christmas. I had three young children.

It was bad enough that they had lost their daddy. I couldn't let Santa die on them, too. So I did the best I could to make things "normal." We decorated the house. We baked cookies shaped like stars and candy canes and bells.

I didn't venture out to buy a Christmas tree until the week before Christmas. It was just too difficult. Maybe it was because I had such vivid memories of the perfect tree we had had the year before, which our friends put up while I was at the hospital, watching Drew slowly slip away from me.

The children and I finally went out one evening and got a tree at the quaint little tree place down the street from our quaint little house. It was a beautiful evening and it was a beautiful tree. The tree people tied it atop our Ford Explorer and off we went, smelling of peppermint and balsam. When we got home, the kids went inside to play and I untied the tree, got the cast iron stand out of its box in the basement, and proceeded to wrestle the tree off the roof of the truck, through the front door, and into the living room.

I had no idea how large that tree was until I had it inside of the house. It was enormous. Undoubtedly the most imposing and unwieldy tree we had ever purchased. As the kids helped me to hoist it into a bucket of fresh water, I realized I'd need to chop a good eight or nine inches off the trunk if we wanted it to stand up beneath our eight-foot, six-inch living room ceiling. So, there I was at ten o'clock at night, with Christmas carols playing on the stereo as I sawed away. It was not an easy feat, but I did it. By the time I got it into the stand, I was sweating like a woman who had just run a marathon, or had been making wild, passionate love for hours on end. Sadly, I couldn't blame my sweatiness on either of those activities.

As I stood back to look at the tree standing there in the corner of the living room, to observe my work, I felt like Superwoman. Or Wonder Woman. Some female superhero with fabulous breasts and a spandex thong. All I know is, it was the biggest tree we ever had, and I had done it all by myself. It was empowering. If I could bury my beloved husband and put up that Christmas tree all within the course of one short year, I could successfully navigate anything life could throw my way.

After quite a bit of untangling, I put all of the many strings of tiny little lights on the tree. It was getting rather late, but I was on a mission. My children were counting on me for some holiday normalcy and I was going to give it to them, dammit. As I attached the final string of lights, the children gathered around, waiting anxiously to be able to hang the ornaments and toss the tinsel around.

I plugged the bottom string into the wall socket, and…nothing. Nothing lit up. Nothing twinkled, blinked, or showed any sign of life. I jiggled things and unplugged and replugged each string, and still, absolutely nothing.

It was then that I lost it. All I remember is tearing strings of lights off an eight-foot-tall balsam fir and swearing. And sobbing. I think that was when my three children ran upstairs and hid under the bed or the computer table or something.

Fortunately, when I fall apart, I am usually able to regain my composure and pull myself back together in relatively short order. I had visions of my poor children sitting in some therapist's office when they were grown up, recounting the story of the Christmas when their newly widowed mother lost her mind.

I didn't want them to have to waste their money paying a therapist to listen to that story.

I was sure they'd have better and more damaging stories to relay to some therapist someday. I mean, I hadn't even started dating in earnest yet—that would certainly give them enough analysis-worthy material.

I went over to the stereo, ripped out Bing Crosby, and popped in a CD entitled *Salsa Around the World*. It was upbeat, fun, made you want to dance and, best of all, had absolutely no connection to Christmas…or to Drew.

Brightened and inspired by the sexy sounds of salsa, I untangled the web of lights and decided to give it another shot. This time, the angels of Christmas illumination intervened and somehow, with just the right combination of patience, love, and reconfiguring, the lights lit, and voilà! Our first tree-without-Drew was awash in sparkle and brilliance.

A new family tradition was born.

Now, every holiday season, in true New England, Norman Rockwell-esque fashion, we decorate the tree while listening to *Salsa Around the World*. This coming year, I plan on having a party, and playing salsa music. And serving margaritas and shots of Cuervo Gold, burritos with mole sauce...and maybe some cookies shaped like jalapeño peppers.

THE WEDDING SHOES

Stop your whining!

I had a neighbor who was very sweet. Sweetness does not always override insensitivity and stupidity, however.

I am thinking in particular of a conversation I had with her in my front yard, about four or five months after Drew died. It was a beautiful sunny day in late spring, and we were making small talk. She had an upcoming wedding to attend and, suddenly, she was sharing with me the horrors and frustrations of finding the right shoes. This poor woman simply could not find shoes that would match her mauve dress. Could I believe it? I mean, she had to go to this wedding, and she had been running around tirelessly, and she still could not find suitable footwear. Even worse, the wedding ceremony was going to be on the beach… and how could she be expected to walk in the sand in high heels?

For goodness sake, did this bride have no idea of the stress and trauma she was causing her female guests?

I just stood there, listening to her, numb. She's lucky I was numb. Had I not been numb, she would have been going to the wedding with not only less-than-perfect shoes but with a black eye, as well.

At that moment, I realized how much I had been changed by Drew's illness and death. The absurdity of that woman's complaints wouldn't have been quite so glaring before all of this had happened to me. In fact, I would have probably stood there and commiserated with her, understanding her plight and having a modicum of empathy.

But at that moment, in addition to wanting to deck her, I also felt like hugging her and saying *thank you!* Because she made me see, so very clearly, how people waste so much time worrying, obsessing, and complaining about things that are miniscule and so unimportant in the grand scheme of our lives.

It struck me as being so sad, and I must admit, I felt sorry for her.

I knew that my experience with Drew had given me a wonderful new perspective. I would never be the same again, and I would never waste a precious moment of my life listening to someone else complaining about something as meaningless and petty as not finding the perfect shoes for a wedding…on the beach, no less.

At the time, I didn't have the emotional energy to tell her that she should have been happy to be going to a wedding on a beautiful beach at sunset on a Saturday evening, with her husband on her arm and her son safe at home with a babysitter.

And I hope she is reading this now, and that she took her shoes off at that wedding and just went barefoot in the sand.

THE VIRGIN SUITE

Fly me to the moon (or maybe just London)

Two-and-a-half years after Drew's death, after we'd moved to Portland, Maine (more on this shortly), I decided to take a trip. Alone. To Europe. I had met a man on an Internet dating site who, having been transplanted from New England to the UK a decade earlier, was planning to be back in the states for a holiday visit with his parents—now conveniently living in Maine. We had met for an enchanting pre–Christmas Eve dinner in Portland, and I'd found him charming (and safe) enough to take him up on his offer to be my most gracious tour guide, should I ever again be inspired to take a trip "across the pond."

My mother most generously, and bravely, agreed to stay with my children for two entire, blissful weeks. The tickets were purchased, and before I knew it, I was off to Boston to catch the first leg of my round-trip adventure. A year or two earlier I might have fantasized about a one-way ticket, but since the move to Maine I was in an increasingly hopeful mood as I peered into my future.

As planned, I spent the first week of my escape, solo, in London, indulging in long, leisurely afternoons at my favorite museums, gardens, and other haunts, before traveling on to Scotland to meet up with my new friend. Once there, the adventure continued. He had been kind enough to arrange for my stay at a lovely, private club (he arranged it, but I was certainly footing the bill), and upon arrival, I was quite appropriately given the key to the room labeled the "Virgin Suite."

Although having had three children and a growing number of post-widowhood sexual experiences clearly meant I was not a virgin, the whole thing struck me as quite perfect. And I appreciated the sense of humor that the owner of the establishment obviously possessed. I'd return from evenings out for wonderful dinners, courtesy of my friend (who had, curiously, not yet even attempted to kiss me) and nights spent flirting with a variety of handsome, foreign-tongued men at the club's private bar, insert my key into the lovely, timeworn door of my Virgin Suite, drop my sexy black pumps or cowboy boots onto the sensual white shag carpeting, and slide into bed, alone, thinking, *This is so fucking cool. Now I remember what it's like to be a woman again! Not a mommy. Not a wife. Not a widow. A* woman.

The trip held many highlights, one of the most memorable being the evening that I found myself seated at the bar beside the club's owner, who had apparently taken a liking to me. Or perhaps, to the way my little widowed behind looked in my jeans (see "My great ass," in chapter nine). Before I knew what was happening, he had sent one of the bartenders to pluck a bottle of champagne, the cost of which was probably equal to a month's heating bill in Maine, and was sitting beside me at the foot of my voluptuous Virgin Suite bed, with two finely cut Swedish crystal glasses in hand.

He was a complete gentleman, and we talked for hours about all manner of things: our children, our creative and business ambitions, and our life's journeys. And by the time we had worked our way through the bottle of champagne, I found myself with an invitation to visit him in Fiji and attend a grand party to celebrate the purchase of his latest home.

And after I gave him a kiss on the cheek goodnight, and after he shut my Virgin Suite door, I once again flopped back onto the virginal, white goose-down comforter and thought, *This is so fucking cool.*

It was just the antidote to my two-plus years of grieving the loss of my husband. Nine days prior, I had been attending a parent-teacher elementary school conference. Today, I was drinking a glass of champagne that cost as much as my weekly grocery bill and getting an invitation to Fiji.

Anything could happen, and the world felt like it once again held endless opportunity. I had begun to find myself once again.

Soon, the black, leather-bound notebooks and sketchbooks I'd brought along on my overseas journey were filled with new ideas and inspiration for the art exhibit I'd later create—along with scribbles of daydreams, hopes, and wishes for a life and a future I thought had long ago been squelched forever.

6
PSYCHOLOGICAL HELP

THE SUPPORT GROUP

Maybe I should have just bought a new underwire bra

I COULDN'T WAIT to go to a support group. It seemed like it would be my salvation. A chance to commiserate with a group of equally miserable and heartbroken people. A chance to talk. A chance to cry. A chance to get out of the house and away from my children for an hour. With the drive back and forth, I could turn it into two hours.

The first support group was an error. I think Drew had been dead for maybe four weeks, and I could barely speak without melting into a puddle of tears.

I listened to everyone else's sad stories, and when it was my turn, I could barely stop weeping long enough to get out two words, much less a complete thought. I had his wedding rings on a chain around my neck, and every time I moved I made this little tinkling sound. Like a cow wearing a cowbell. A couple of the women came up to me as we walked to the elevator after the meeting and told me what a sweet idea that was. My cowbell.

"Oh, look Gladys…she has his wedding rings on a necklace. Isn't that a sweet idea?"

They were probably twenty years older than me, had no children at home to care for, and had lost their husbands years ago. They were still going to a grief support group. I knew one thing: I did not want to be them. I went home and took off the cowbell shortly thereafter.

The second support group was not an error—it was a learning experience.

I don't know that I learned much about grieving or how to get through the ordeal I was going through. I did, however, learn that even in the midst of gut-wrenching tragedy, I really did enjoy public speaking. Here I was, widowed for maybe four months, and I was sitting in a depressing and dismal room on a folding chair. With a bunch of strangers. Making them laugh.

As with the first attempt, my motivations for joining were varied. This time, however, my priorities had shifted slightly. I looked at it first and foremost as an opportunity for an evening out. Once a week! I would get to talk. I would get to talk. I would get to talk. I would get to entertain people and make people laugh. I had an audience. I also got to cry and commiserate with others who were miserable. But the difference was that I no longer saw them as equally miserable.

Let me rephrase that. I no longer saw myself as being in an

equal state of misery with most of them. In fact, the support group really boosted my self-esteem and my optimism. I was in a room with people who had lost their spouses one, two, even three years ago! This was inconceivable to me. I mean, I couldn't imagine still wanting or needing a support group that far down the road. And these people were still crying and floundering, unable to move on with their lives. Not all of them, but a good percentage of them.

I felt rather sorry for them. I felt sorry for them because they had forgotten how to laugh. I knew I wouldn't ever forget how to laugh. I felt better off than them, even if I did have three children to raise all by myself. At least I could find the humor in my situation, and in life.

Even the facilitator seemed depressed…and she was still married to a man who was alive.

I decided then and there that I was somehow, luckily, above the fray. Despite my bad luck, I felt fortunate. Well, almost. I would get dressed up nicely (which at the time meant that I had remembered to put on clean underwear and possibly even some perfume, although things like mascara were still out of the question; see the earlier story on tissue lint). Plus, I was like the star of the support group: I made people smile. I made people feel better. I even made some people feel more fortunate about their circumstances. I mean, I had been left alone with three young children. I loved them with all of my heart. But as a grieving, forty-one-year-old single woman, from a logistical standpoint, I was in a stifling, suburban, Stepford-wife-ish hell.

At least those other women could go out and cry into their coffee with a girlfriend, or escape for a nice dinner and a glass of wine when they felt the need, without having to not only pro-cure a decent babysitter but also pay her twelve dollars an hour.

I was almost sad when the eight-week-long support group stint ended. Although the triple-digit admission fee felt extremely insensitive and cruel to me (*How could anyone make grieving people pay money to sit around and cry together?*), by the last ses-sion, I was really in my element. Our assignment for that last week was to gather things at home that you would bring in for a "show and tell" style thing. Memorabilia that represented your late spouse, so everyone could get a glimpse into who they were. I went home after we got our instructions and it was like I had gotten this great college project to work on. I found things that screamed "Drew" to me. Antique tin sand toys, funny cards he had given me, goofy photos of him and the kids, romantic gifts, everything that reflected so clearly who he was.

When it was my turn to do my little "presentation," I feared a breakdown of massive proportions. I imagined I'd end up cry-ing, with a river of tears preventing me from speaking. But I did just fine, and managed to laugh, cry, and tell everyone about my wonderful husband. I felt as if I was presenting a campaign to a client at an ad agency—selling Drew. He was a hit, and I was a hit. I made everyone laugh, I made everyone cry.

Lord knows, I was not going to be attending a support group three years down the road. Being paid to run one, maybe. But paying money to attend one? No way. I was moving on to bigger and better things. I was going to stop commiserating, get the tissue lint off my eyelashes, and figure out who I was, without Drew.

Well…maybe not quite yet.

ANTIDEPRESSANTS

I imagine there comes a time in every grief-stricken woman's life when the idea of going on antidepressants becomes rather appealing. I am not a person who likes to take much of anything but the occasional dose of Nyquil when I'm sick once or twice each winter, and maybe my daily vitamin regimen. But after spending a few weeks with a tear-stained face and clothing with soggy collars and three children to look after twenty-four hours a day—even I began to think the world of antidepressants was one I might want to be a part of.

It didn't really hit me that it was possibly my only hope for temporary happiness until about a year and a half after Drew died. It was July, and we were heading down to our favorite town in Cape Cod for two weeks of beautiful fun-in-the-sun beach vacation. Me, my three children, and my mother. Not me, my three children, and Drew. Not me, my three children, Drew, and my mother. But just me, my three children, and my mother.

I didn't realize how sad it made me until about a week before we were due to pack up and leave. The thought of going back to a place that held so many wonderful memories—two-parent, three-child memories—made me feel ill.

So I did the only thing I could think of doing, short of crawling into my bed and staying there with the air conditioning on until it was time to go back to school. I went to my doctor and asked her for a prescription for something. Anything to put a half-inch cushion between myself and my new widowed reality.

She wondered why I hadn't asked earlier, given my circumstances. I wondered why I hadn't asked earlier, either. And thus began my foray into the world of "happy pills." I got a few sample packs to last me for the two-week vacation. They weren't even the normal-sized dosage but teeny-tiny mini little micro pills. I took one as soon as I got out of her office and into my car and could find the bottle of water that my kids had left wedged under the car seat. Thankfully, it still had a few sips left in it because I couldn't wait one more second to feel less pain. Less sadness. Less despair. Less ambivalence about life.

Everything was going well. We packed up and left for the beach a few days later. I took my little happy pill faithfully, every morning. I won't mention any specific brand; I will only say that the commercial on television featured a round little smiley-faced bubble that represented "you on this antidepressant."

About a week or so into our vacation, I noticed something was different. Was I feeling happier and more jubilant? No, that wasn't it. What I was feeling was tired. Because I was waking up at about three o'clock each morning and not getting back to sleep until the sun came up. Just in time for my kids to come in an hour or two later and jump in my bed, begging to go to the beach.

I was also noticing something else. I was suddenly, decidedly, well...how can I say this? Smelly. Yes, I was smelly. Gassy and smelly. And after a while, even my children (and you know how smelly they can be) would open the door to my bedroom after I had been locked in there all night and exclaim, "Wow, Mom... is that *you?*" Their little hands flailing through the air as they simultaneously pinched their noses.

For two days I racked my brain, trying to think of what I was eating or drinking that could be having such a horrible effect on me. Was it the clams? Was it the water? I finally came to the conclusion that the only thing I had been doing differently was taking those innocuous-looking pills. The ones with that little happy-go-lucky smiling picture on the commercial. As it turns out, that cute, little, round, smiling bubble icon on the commercial was not just a happy face. It was a gas bubble. A smelly, smiley, stinky gas bubble. Thank God I have a sense of humor. Because I finally just sat there and laughed.

Yes, those little antidepressants might have eventually kicked in and made me feel a bit lighter, but they would also (clearly) make me into a virtual man-repellent. I weighed my options:

OK, I can either be happy and never have sex again or be in a state of low-grade depression for a while longer, but smell pleasant enough to have a man still want to be near me.

There was no choice. I ditched the pills and remained sad. The hot sex with the handsome guy I was dating a couple of weeks later helped cheer me up considerably, however.

FIRE THAT THERAPIST

Before and after Drew's death, I sought the advice of a number of very qualified professional therapists. A diagnosis of terminal cancer is stressful, to say the least, and can put a terrible strain on an otherwise perfectly imperfect marriage. And support from a healthcare professional seemed crucial at certain junctures, when our world was crashing down around us. Sometimes we went in tandem, sometimes we went alone, all in an effort to deal with the ways in which this nightmare was affecting us both as individuals and as a couple.

After Drew's death, I sought help for obvious reasons—the main one being that I didn't think I could keep getting out of bed every day and moving on with my life without a solid team of people cheering me on and helping me sort through the tangle of sadness, fears, insecurities, hopes, and frustrations that filled my mind and my heart.

So, although I undoubtedly paid a handsome price for the help I so desperately sought, I only recall a handful of occasions upon which any of the therapists I bankrolled did or said something that made a truly positive impact on me. And admittedly, this caused me to feel a bit of unhealthy resentment each time I'd adorn yet another check with my signature.

One of my favorite "therapy memories" was provided to me by the woman I shall call Therapist B. At the time, I was contemplating moving my family to Maine, and at one point felt very excited that I was finally a hundred percent certain that I wanted to sell my house and take a large step forward toward my future. The same house I would be selling was the one where Drew had died two years earlier, and I felt as if I'd served my sentence and needed to move on or risk losing my sanity. My mantra at the time was an optimistic and reassuring Zen Buddhist saying: "Leap and the net shall appear."

When I enthusiastically shared my plan with the therapist (whose husband was, by the way, at work with his own patients upstairs, in their multimillion dollar home in a pricey suburb of Boston), she looked at me with a solemn expression and stated dryly, "Well, at least that's what you hope will happen."

A hundred dollars an hour…and that's the kind of professional wisdom I'm receiving?

The fact that, despite moments during some of our sessions when she appeared to be in some sort of self-induced trance (or maybe just hadn't had enough sleep the night before), she was always alert enough to cut me off midsentence when our forty-nine minutes and fifty-nine seconds were up, made her lack of support all the more annoying. And I had to wonder whether her apparent lack of enthusiasm for my plan to move had something to do with the fact that I'd no longer be on her weekly appointment calendar.

And how did that make me feel, you ask?

Angry!

There, I said it.

I fired her immediately, put my house on the market in short order, and moved to the coast of Maine. And, by the way, I was right about the net.

My second-favorite therapist story occurred earlier, approximately seventeen months after Drew's death, and was provided by Therapist A. At that time, I found myself dating a man who was handsome, charming, and felt like a wonderful fit on many levels. But for the fact that he wasn't much of an email writer, I found him to be quite perfect. It wasn't that he couldn't string together words in a meaningful fashion, it was that as soon as any little thing would go awry between us, he would stop emailing. As a form of punishment. Some people withhold sex when there are bumps in the relationship road. He withheld words on a computer screen. If we were having a little tiff, his emails would get shorter and shorter. At one point, he responded to a heartfelt outpouring of emotion from me with a five-word response. This was the first time I ever recall wanting to cause physical harm to anyone by reaching through a computer screen.

For many, the email thing wouldn't be such a sore spot, but I am a woman who cherishes written expression. He also lived a hundred miles away, and we both had children whose presence kept us from having a lot of phone time. Which meant that at times the written word was all we had to keep the magic alive.

As our days of long-distance dating turned into weeks, and then months, I realized that his idea of communication just wasn't doing it for me. But the fact that we couldn't keep our hands off one another when we were together left me in a quandary as to how to proceed. And so, off to the therapist du jour I went. Clearly, I had too much free time on my hands. And, at the time, too much spare cash.

Therapist A was actually the same therapist who had been a sounding board for Drew and me during his illness, and she knew my emotional history quite well. So when I explained my situation with this man, of whom I was quite enamored, and our communication issue, I was amazed and quite undelighted as I listened to her professional advice, which by my calculation was no bargain at nearly two dollars per minute:

> *Well, Sandi, how are you going to mourn the loss of the emails you will never be receiving from this man?*

The timer went off. I wrote her a check. And as I walked to my car, the following belated reply went through my head:

Mourn? The loss? Of cyberspace communiqués? Are you kidding me?! I'll tell you how I'm going to "mourn the fucking loss," sweetheart: I'm going to dump him!

I had lost a husband. I knew what it meant to truly *mourn*. And her use of this word in relation to an emotionally incompetent man's refusal to do the one small thing that brought me great happiness flipped a switch inside my still rather recently widowed self.

And that is how I ended up with Therapist B. And you already know how that ended.

SELF-HELP BOOKS, MY ASS!

How many self-help books can one woman own, much less read? In my case, enough for a really good bonfire.

After my husband died, I did what many widows do: I cried, I swore, and I searched for support. I eventually ended up in the self-help aisle of every major book-selling establishment in the greater Boston area. I am reticent to admit the number of do-it-yourself-fix-me-please books I accumulated. The stack next to my bed grew higher and higher, in proportion to my Kleenex pile.

There were books written by widows, by therapists, by widows who were therapists, by clergymen (and clergywomen), and by widows and widowers who were therapists and/or clergypeople, and had ended up in connubial bliss. Together. God knows how this happened, and how these people got so fortunate as to find one another. I apparently should have been ordained, secured a degree in psychology, or at the very least, gotten my MSW before Drew died on me.

All I wanted was to find something penned by a woman with three kids, a dead husband, a variety of pets, a mortgage, and the libido of a college frat boy.

Initially, I limited my collection solely to books with the word *grief* in the title. As the months went by, I slowly expanded into titles that included *dating*. In the end, none of them really helped. Most of them just served to annoy, irritate, and depress me. Especially the ones written by the people who didn't actually have a dead spouse of their very own. Having a nice little degree is one thing, but watching someone throw dirt atop the coffin of your soulmate is another thing entirely. I wanted someone with experience. Not college credits. And, despite the fact that I didn't consider myself a writer at the time, I realized right then that I'd eventually need to write my own book if I ever wanted to truly heal my heart.

There was only one book that inspired me, and made me feel that there was a reason not to join my husband six feet under. I didn't find it at Barnes and Noble—I found it at the town transfer station (a nice, twenty-first-century term for "dump").

It was in the swap-shop area, and it wasn't even about widowhood. Written by a woman who had tragically lost a young-adult son, it was the only book with a title that contained a hint of the humor that lay within. In another fine example of the ways in which the great "circle of life" generally works, the book itself landed back at the swap shop of another town, after we moved to Maine, so I cannot share said title with you. Because I don't remember it. But I can tell you it was the only book that made me smile, in between my tears. This woman understood that grief doesn't take away one's personality or one's ability to find humor in things. Even desperately dark things.

And believe me, that was precisely what I needed to keep me waking up each day. A bit of humor, and the promise that one day, my stomach muscles would, once again, ache. Not from sobbing, but from laughing.

7

DATING AND SEX 101

DEATH AND DATING

A FEW WEEKS BEFORE Drew died, we were lying beside one another on our bed.

It would turn out to be the last time we would ever share that bed and make love.

Drew had been in and out of the hospital for an overnight here and there over the course of the previous weeks, and was in a downward spiral that we didn't want to acknowledge. Not really. Ever hopeful, we just kept moving ahead. Doing the next procedure, and the next…and the next. He had tubes coming out of his sides, and his body was failing. I imagine he must have been miserable, but he never let anyone know just how bad it was.

Especially not me.

On that evening, he said the only thing he would ever say to me that indicated he thought he might not make it through this ordeal. I remember him lying beside me, gently holding my hand as he told me he wanted me to have another man in my life... after he was gone. That he wanted me to have someone to love and cherish me, and to be there for our children.

I could barely look him in the eyes as he spoke. The unarticulated ache that permeated the air between us made me feel as if I were breathing cement.

And for the first time in our thirty-three months of cautious hopefulness, I felt as if we were losing the battle. And that I was losing him.

In a final act of selflessness, he also told me he wanted me to have "my store." He broke down in tears when he said those words. He knew that my dream had always been to have my own shop somewhere, filled with my art and funky antiques and wonderfully quirky, sentimental things to make people smile. That dream no longer existed in my life after the first doctor breathed the words *pancreatic cancer*, but Drew loved and shared my creative spirit, and understood the depth and importance of my dreams.

He was dying, and all he cared about was that I fall in love again, fulfill my creative potential, and follow the dreams that he knew still lived somewhere in my heart.

Not every widow knows that her husband would have wanted her to fall in love again. Sometimes it's because the death is sudden and there is no chance to talk; other times it's because the man is selfish, and doesn't really, truly want to imagine he will be replaced. I've heard stories like that, of men who, while on their deathbed, actually told their wives that they didn't want them to ever marry again.

I cannot even imagine living with those words. Luckily, I didn't have to.

So here I am, dating. Again. Just like when I was 17. Only this time, my three children are along for the ride. The four of us are dating, actually.

Now, may I just take this opportunity to say that dating while simultaneously missing your deceased husband and raising three children isn't the most desirable of situations. Just as grieving, dating, and single parenting are not standard elements of a successful fairytale. Cinderella did not meet Prince Charming at a grief support group while their seven combined children sat at home with their respective babysitters.

Let's get real.

Over the years, it's been difficult for me to date anyone while holding back my feelings and admitting, at least to myself, how much I still miss Drew, and how much I really just want him back. I realize that knowledge can't possibly make any new men in my life feel especially confident, knowing—even if it's never said—that they're with someone who would honestly prefer to still be with a man who's no longer alive. But it's my reality. It's the blessing and curse of having loved someone so completely.

It's also the blessing and curse of being widowed, rather than divorced.

WIDOWED, NOT DIVORCED

There is a difference between being widowed and being divorced, and it's a significant one. I know plenty of divorced women. The difference between most of them and me is that, although a good number of them went through hell, their hell has a name: Bob or Bill or Jim or Richard.

If they're really unfortunate, their hell has the nickname Dick.

Now, being widowed, I went through hell too. According to the life stressor charts, a 33 percent more horrendous version of hell. But my hell doesn't live and breathe with his second wife in a four bedroom Colonial twenty minutes away. My hell was due to a bunch of pancreatic cells run amuck, and the fact that I was still madly in love with my husband. In fact, his being ill just made me love him more—more deeply, more tenderly, more passionately. It made me appreciate all of his wonderful qualities, and reminded me why I fell in love with him in the first place. Why I married him. So, by the time he died two-and-a-half years after his diagnosis, I was more in love with him than the day we first met.

You don't hear many divorced women telling you how much more they loved and appreciated their exes after the court proceedings were over and the custody agreement was signed.

So although both divorcees and widows can be found dating while raising children, divorcees are not, for the most part, simultaneously pining away for their husbands. They may be missing their snow-shoveling capabilities, or the way they could make the toilet stop running in the middle of the night. But rarely do they miss their ex in a romantic way. They have usually built up a sufficient amount of dislike, disappointment, and/or bitterness during the course of the separation and divorce to propel them safely into the world of dating. Most of my divorced acquaintances are not longing for husband number one. He was not Prince Charming. That is why they're divorced. They can move on. And not only can they often move on sooner, but they usually get to have sex a lot sooner and more frequently, too. As I write this, I have been widowed for a number of years. Last year, I had sex three times. Sadly, it wasn't even great sex. And I am in the prime of my life.

Although I don't envy the divorced population, I would sometimes give anything to have an ex who would take my kids every Wednesday night and every other weekend—if only to afford me the opportunity to be violated in any room I might desire. In my own house.

In my current situation, sex can only be had in a rented hotel room, or elsewhere if I'm lucky enough to have stumbled upon a man who has his own house and meets one of the following criteria:

- no children

- grown children

- children of whom he has only partial custody

Otherwise, my only remaining options are the reenactment of certain college liaisons involving cars and an outdoor locale, or embarking upon a romantic encounter in my own home and risking the very real probability of a child intruding at an inopportune moment.

As I said, dating with a dead husband and children in tow is not the ideal situation.

I must confess, however, to the fact that on some level, I still consider myself lucky. I would rather have a dead husband who adored me and who treated me with respect and love than an ex-husband who cheated on me with the twenty-one-year-old Swedish nanny.

SEVEN MONTHS, TWENTY-SIX DAYS

...and counting

Journal entry

> 22 August 2003
>
> 2:30 a.m., Friday
>
> My Love,
>
> It is almost eight months since you left me, and still my tears keep streaming down my cheeks. I miss you— that's all there is to it. I miss you and love you and I don't know how to stop missing you and loving you so damned much. Sorry about the swearing.
>
> Nothing makes it go away. I almost feel ready to go out on a date with a guy.... but what I really want is someone to hold me and kiss me and drive me wild with desire, the way you did. I miss that. Last August 13th was

the day you had your scan and we found out the bad news about your recurrence. That was pretty much the end of our days of semi-carefree kissing and lovemaking. So, here I am, a year later, and I feel so physically deprived. I talked with T last night (really late) and also to J (even later!).

It was so great to just talk to some *men*.

I am so tired of constantly talking with women.

J and I were joking about how totally "shallow" we both are...as far as physical attraction goes. As he said, "You had Drew—of course your standards are going to be high!" I just totally have to have someone tall, dark, and handsome. I find myself daydreaming and fantasizing about one guy after another. I feel like some sort of nymphomaniac.

I am so sex-starved. *Help!*

Please send someone to me, soon. And would you please be in more of my dreams....I never seem to dream about you often enough for my liking.

I miss you, my lover.

Forever,

Sandi

SEVEN MONTHS, TWENTY-SEVEN DAYS

...and counting

23 August 2003

Saturday, 10 p.m.

How depressing...Saturday night and here I am at ten o'clock writing in my journal about how depressed I am. I guess *deprived* would be the correct word.

So I feel like I might just be the horniest woman alive. I honestly feel this kind of panic, almost. Like I will just explode, or implode, or something, if I do not have physical contact with a member of the male species sometime soon. I "satisfy" myself constantly, but it isn't the same at all. Duh. Anyway, when I think of Drew and his tight little black (or white) Ralph Lauren Polo underwear or those tight little Calvin Klein numbers or (last and best of all) those stretchy Donna Karan sexy boxers...I just want to honestly *weep!* I mean, he was like some super-sexy underwear model. I would give anything to walk into my bedroom tonight and find him stretched out there, smelling of Armani cologne, waiting for me with his dark, thick, wavy hair still slicked back and wet from a shower.

I will never again in my life take sex for granted. Once I find the right man (again), I will have sex like there really is no tomorrow, because now I truly know from experience that there very well might not be. Drew had a lot of tomorrows after his diagnosis and surgery (about 978 of them, give or take a few)...but the word *cancer* tainted those tomorrows.

We made love plenty of times in those 978 days, but it wasn't the same as before. There was a tinge of sadness to it…of melancholy. At least that's how I felt. We all go through life so foolishly. Taking every day for granted, and it's all so unbelievably unfair.

I am 41…probably just hitting my sexual prime, or so I'm told. I feel beautiful and confident and in really great shape. I have an IUD with a lot of years left on it. I don't have any little, tiny, helpless babies anymore, and am not nursing or being spit up on or changing poopy diapers…and now I have no one to have sex with. How depressing is *that?!*

Drew must be up in heaven, smiling that devilish, sexy, million-dollar smile of his and saying,

See sweetie, I told you we should have had more sex.

Yes, my love, we sure #*!@ing should have.

EIGHT MONTHS

…and counting

26 August 2003

5:10 p.m.

I know it is eight months today that Drew died, and this probably isn't appropriate, but I am so infatuated with this guy who works at the garden center. He's tall, dark, handsome, nice body. I have butterflies in my stomach when I think about him. Of course, he's probably married, but God, I can only pray that he isn't.

I noticed him when we first moved to town, when I went in there a lot last spring and summer. When I think of him, I get goosebumps, and when I actually spoke with him on the phone today, I realized what a sexy phone voice he has. He can't be gay, can he? No, a gay guy doing "manly" work at a garden place? No. Couldn't be. I don't know, I just know I told him I'd be in next week to talk with him some more about firewood and Norfolk pine trees.

Oh well, whatever, at least it gives me hope that there *are* men out there who still turn me on. Maybe if he's married, or gay, or both, he has a brother.

Send me a guy, sweetie, I can't take this celibacy much longer…or at least send me someone who's a great kisser!

PREPARING TO DATE

*Fasten your seatbelt, and please note the location
of the nearest emergency exit*

I clearly remember the day I knew I was ready to start dating. It had been eight-and-a-half months since Drew's death. It was a sultry late-summer's day, and I could think of nothing but sex.

And then I started to panic. I started to feel as if I had better jump back into the dating pond and kiss a frog soon, or my lips might forget how to kiss. Permanently.

This also led me to realize that kissing would (with any luck) lead to having sex. And if I wanted to ever, ever, ever have sex... it could not involve any underwear that was presently taking up space in my dresser drawers. I could absolutely not have great sex with any other man if I was wearing underwear that Drew had seen, purchased, nibbled on, fondled, or torn off of my body at any time.

Which segues nicely into my next (practical) topic: underwear.

THE UNDERWEAR OVERHAUL

Going up, third floor, lingerie

It was time for a complete lingerie revamp. A metamorphosis. A renewal. Out with the old, in with the new. I went through my drawers, tossed most of what I had, saved a few things for sentimental reasons (presumably to wear when I really wanted to be miserable and have a good cry and was missing Drew immensely. Like on Valentine's Day, our anniversary, etc.). I then headed off to an upscale department store and started over from scratch.

I got off the elevator with just the bra and panties on my back and got back on with a selection of lingerie to rival Imelda Marcos's shoe collection.

Breathless from time in the fitting room spent wrestling with all manner of hooks, snaps, ties, buttons, loops, and corsetry, I plunked down my pile of goodies on the countertop in front of the cashier. Though *plunked* is not quite the right word. It was more like dropping a pile of feathers. Lingerie doesn't weigh much. The saleslady was a sweet, older woman who complimented me on my exquisite taste—and then asked why I was buying out half the lingerie department.

I gave her a short summary of my sad tale of widowhood, and with dewy eyes, she smiled sweetly and said, "Well you *should* be dating again and having sex. You're a beautiful young woman!"

That saleslady made my day. I left there that evening feeling like I was, indeed, going to have a life, even without Drew. And, dear saleslady, if you're reading this and if you remember me from the lingerie department at that store just outside of Boston, Massachusetts, on an early autumn night in 2003, thank you for your kind words and vote of confidence.

It gave me hope and spurred me onward.

SEXUAL HEALING

So beginning about eight months after I buried Drew, I spent the next five years (at least) using dating and sex in a desperate attempt to heal the hole in my heart and the hurt that permeated my being. Of course, it took me a good number of additional years to recognize that's what I'd been doing.

I remember one of the first men I dated asking me, both quizzically and fearfully, "But how do you know you're ready to date?

Your husband has only been dead for nine months."

Of course, I would assure any man asking this question that I simply knew that I was ready. In reality, I was thinking, *Of course I'm ready. I haven't had sex since December of 2002. And I'm tired of spending every evening at home, with my children. No matter how cute they are.*

Admittedly, I wasn't really dating. I was conducting an experiment. To see if someone could even begin to take Drew's place in my life. To see if anyone could make my heart ache a bit less. I was searching for mind-numbing kissing and coma-inducing sex with someone who wouldn't expect too much else of me, emotionally speaking. I was testing the waters, getting ready for the day when I might be ready to jump in with both feet again.

Admittedly, I left a string of poor, unsuspecting, often-confused men in my wake—not that they were all wonderful specimens of dating fabulousness, or that many of them didn't deserve their fate. It's simply that every man is the wrong man when you're not really ready for a relationship. He can, however, be oh-so-right for meaningless, shallow sex. If you can keep it meaningless. Which I, like many women, thought I could do, but oftentimes could not.

And so I'd sometimes start out of the gate wanting "meaning-less," get a tiny bit emotionally attached, and then feel angry that they weren't making my heart skip a beat. Yes, I kept trying to turn Mr. Wrong into Mr. Right. A nip here, a tuck there. I didn't want to turn them into Drew, but I wanted to turn them into someone who made me feel the way Drew had made me feel. Of course, this was generally not a successful endeavor.

As they say, if you want an apple, don't climb a pear tree.

I tried not to put Drew up on a pedestal. I tried to remember that we had a perfectly imperfect marriage. I reminded myself of his faults, like the way he'd leave wet towels on the floor or dirty socks in the den. But even with his obviously irritatingly charming faults, he was still the best thing I'd ever stumbled upon in this life of mine.

Romantically speaking, that is.

When you're dating and in your forties, there are really only three men out there to date: the divorced guy, the widowed guy, and the most evil of all, the eternal bachelor. I have found there is no such thing as a forty-something-year-old man who hasn't been married and is really commitment material. Typically, I'd take a divorced guy over the never-married variety any day.

So as a widow, I don't have problems with divorced guys. Unless, of course, they tell me their divorce was based upon some seemingly juvenile reason such as we just couldn't get along. I do have one caveat—if a man is divorced due to an affair with a babysitter or secretary, his inability to deal with fatherhood, or the fact that he wanted his wife to get breast implants and she refused—well, gee, it's just not going to work for me.

I need someone who understands pain and heartache. Preferably, someone who's been broken to the depths of their soul, the way I have. Someone I can respect.

And a divorce of the "stupid" variety just isn't going to make me feel as if we're on equal footing.

Sorry.

So after years of dating and compiling data, I've realized that most of my widowed dating experiences with men can be broken down into these basic categories:

- gay men who apparently don't yet know they're gay

- men who have never been married and who say they want to be in a committed relationship, but have not yet looked up the word *committed* in a dictionary

- divorced men who have a kooky ex-wife I don't want to be tethered to by association

- men who haven't an inkling about what true heartache is, and so, cannot possibly understand the depth of mine

- men who have their shrink's number on speed-dial, and/or have an unhealthy attachment to their mother

- men who are humor-deficient

In conclusion, I can state with great assuredness that all of those early years of rather reckless, sex-centric dating were akin to a research project, and did, indeed, help me to heal. Those dinner dates, mystery meetings over a glass of cabernet, and evenings of urgent and sizzling-hot lovemaking filled parts of my empty time, soothed parts of my broken heart, and kept me from going insane.

The orgasms didn't hurt either, and raised my endorphin level considerably.

INTERNET COURTSHIP

I would eventually like to be in love with a new man. However, finding this new man is a process that hasn't proven to be easy. When I first began dating, all I needed was a warm body. I needed comfort. And someone, pretty much anyone, who was fun and kind and seemed to care about me would do. I was in mourning. And I was feeling very, very alone and very, very sad.

Since I was widowed while still young enough to care whether I ever went on a dinner date again, but not of the personality to hang out alone, perched on a barstool, looking for a possibly inebriated soulmate number two, I found myself immersed in the brave new world of Internet courtship.

The budding author in me thoroughly enjoyed the writing component of online dating, although the emails I received in reply to my wondrous musings were a mixed bag—some unbelievably beautiful and touching, and some just plain unbelievable. I'd say the ratio of "wonderful" to something that fell between "mediocre and dreadful" was approximately one to ten.

It sometimes made me laugh, and it sometimes depressed me further, making me long for the days when male "suitors" wrote lengthy, lovely letters to the objects of their affection… with fountain pens. On heavyweight, cotton-linen blend paper. A watermark in the corner, and perhaps a dog-eared black-and-white photograph tucked in for good measure.

GAINING PERSPECTIVE

It took me many false starts, but after approximately half a decade (what I now lovingly refer to as my "five years of angry dating"), I was finally able to put the whole relationship thing in perspective, for the most part, and truly, happily focus on my art, my writing, and the things that bring me creative fulfillment.

I think that, for me, I just needed to get so exhausted, bored, and frustrated by the entire dating process that it was easier to just finally do something else with the bulk of my free time.

In short, I was dated out.

Much like an addict in recovery, I have, of course, had many relapses and times when I've fallen off of the wagon and tried to fill the void in my soul with shallow little pseudo-relationships and pseudo-meaningful sex. But I always bounce back a little more quickly, and a little stronger. I know now that those titillating men sporting lightweight Italian suits or those bad boy types wanting me to hop on the back of their motorcycle aren't really the answer to my happiness. Sexy? Perhaps. Exciting? Perhaps. But not the answer.

They are only a temporary detour, leading me back to my creativity…and to my true north.

And now that I'm back, I'm staying here.

I DON'T WANT YOUR HUSBAND—*REALLY*

When your husband dies and you are still relatively young and, some might say, relatively sexy, you quickly find out that certain other women are threatened by you. But they feel guilty about feeling threatened by you, because your husband wasn't some jerk who deserted you...no, your husband just went and died.

Being a widow is very different from being a divorcee. In addition to the ways I've already mentioned, as a widow, you receive a lot of sympathy and empathy, and no one talks behind your back about what a pity it is that your marriage couldn't work out. No one gossips about who cheated on whom or who slept with the babysitter, or who is or isn't going to pay alimony.

A widow is seen as decidedly more pure and innocent and helpless, even if we widows are, for the most part, not at all pure or innocent or helpless. That's the perception, however. Especially by the living, breathing, male population.

Suddenly, men are everywhere. They want to shovel your snow, mow your lawn, and fix your pipes. I don't mean to imply any sort of sexual innuendo here. I mean, men really want to fix your pipes.

Of course, when you are exhausted from crying twenty-four/ seven while trying to take care of three sad children, you are happy to allow anyone to do anything for you. And this is where you can see who your real women friends are. Your true friends will let their husbands fix your pipes without worrying that those husbands will end up in bed with you in a few months, one afternoon while your kids are in school.

On the other hand, women who are of lesser confidence, and

also not your true friends, will try to keep their husbands as far from you (and your snow, lawn, pipes) as possible.

I will never forget the day one of my then ten-year-old daughter's little girlfriends came to our house for a playdate. Her father delivered her to the door, and I invited him to step inside. I had never met him before. He said hello and we exchanged an awkward greeting. Everyone always felt awkward. No man knows what to say after your husband has died—especially when they are the same age and are secretly wondering whether their number might be coming up next.

So we exchanged thirty seconds of pleasantries, and then out spilled an offer to come to my aid should I ever need help with anything around the house. Though our daughters were friends, I didn't know the man, and was quite touched by the gesture. I thought, *What a sweet man, and what good friends we have here in this town. Especially since we've only lived here for a year.*

The next day, while speaking with his wife on the phone, I made mention of her husband's generous offer. I think I said something like, "It was nice to finally meet Ralph, and it was so sweet that he offered to help me if I need anything fixed around the house."

To which she replied in a shocked voice, "He did?"

I could tell he would not be over to fix any of my leaky pipes anytime soon. Apparently, he was not even doing a very good job of taking care of the pipes at home.

Now, this man was not particularly handsome or studly. He did not look like Brad Pitt or George Clooney, and he didn't have a sparkling personality. I have met plenty of *real* plumbers, electricians, and handymen who were more alluring. Yet, this man's poor wife was afraid I was going to break up their happy home and steal him, or something of the sort.

I wanted to show her a photo of my dear, departed, handsome husband and say, *Hello! Let's get real here.*

I suddenly realized the power I now had. I felt like a black widow spider. Waiting to pounce on some insecure, unsuspecting suburban housewife's paunchy, balding, boring, middle-aged husband and spin him into my web. So I could feed him to my kids for dinner.

Well, it would have been more nutritious than the chicken in potato chip crumbs that the neighbor dropped off for us, I suppose.

THE PLUMBER AND THE PANTIES

About seven months after Drew died we had a minor plumbing disaster. It was August, and we were one short day away from leaving on our two-week vacation to our friends' farmhouse in the idyllic mountains of Vermont. The mere fact that I was going away for two weeks alone with three children, without any other adult to accompany me including Drew, was a big deal.

Our washing machine's decision to break just as I was about to do mountains of pretrip laundry turned out to be an even bigger deal.

I was fortunate enough to procure the name of a good plumber from a neighborhood friend. I was even more fortunate to learn that, after hearing my tale of woe, he was willing to come over the next morning. It turned out that he was not only a plumber, but a plumber whose wife had died. A plumber who was raising two young children, by himself.

This information, relayed during a brief phone conversation with said plumber propelled me into a state of panic. A man was coming over to my house. A single, grief-stricken man, who knew that I was single and grief-stricken, too. It was a tiny bit exciting, and more than a tiny bit terrifying. When he rang my doorbell the next day, I felt like my prom date had just arrived to pick me up.

As it turned out, there was something stuck in the pipe. In the drainpipe of our basement utility sink, which was next to the washing machine. Whenever we'd run the washing machine the water couldn't drain properly because it was connected to that sink drain.

I have forgotten the precise sequence of events, but I do recall the plumber wanting to come back to unclog the drain so my washing machine could work once again. I also recall lying in my bed the night before we were to leave for Vermont and having an epiphany. I suddenly knew precisely why that drain was clogged—my mother had been visiting and, having found the basement sink filled with an assortment of panties that I had left soaking in there in Woolite, had tried to finish rinsing them for me, pulled the rubber plug, and *whoops!*, a few of my finest thongs were lost in action.

When I remembered that little scene I realized that I could not, under any circumstances, have the plumber/widower come over to unclog my drain and then yank out a wisp of a lacy black thong as I stood beside him, feigning surprise.

So I did what any woman who was scared to death of any level of intimacy with a man other than her husband would do. I made up some delaying excuse and set off on the four hour drive to Vermont with my children. But I left a key so he could fix the clog after I was at a safe distance.

That distance being two hundred miles.

Now the story gets even better. The plumber called me in Vermont the next evening and he told me he had fixed my washer. He'd fixed my pipes. My sink. And all of my worldly problems. He told me that I wouldn't believe what the problem actually turned out to be. I said I could not possibly even take a guess. Then he informed me he had discovered some underwear in the drain.

"Really?" I gasped. "You're kidding!"

I thanked him immensely for solving the washing machine mystery and offered to mail him a check. When he turned that down, I offered to send him a bottle of wine for his valiant plumbing efforts instead.

He countered with a suggestion that he take me out for a drink. I froze, like Bambi in the headlights. Thank goodness I was two hundred miles away and on the other end of a phone line instead of in his line of vision.

I politely declined. I am certain I laughed nervously and made some silly comment. Thankfully, I don't remember. My widowed psyche has most graciously allowed me to erase that part.

All I know is, when I returned home with my children from our two-week hiatus, there was no trace of the aforementioned undergarments lying next to the now unclogged utility sink. And for the next year, I drove around town wondering whether one day I would come across his plumber's truck, parked at the local grocery store…my panties dangling from his rearview mirror.

MY SHRINKING SOULMATE

I don't believe that we all have only one soulmate. Were this true, I would have given up completely after Drew died and would now probably be living in seclusion somewhere in the woods. Wearing Birkenstocks.

So, the way I see it, I had soulmate number 1.

He died.

When I started dating again in 2003, I wrote up the requisites for soulmate number 2. It was a "perfect man" list that took up four notebook pages. College ruled.

By 2011 my requirements had been boiled down to five essentials and fit onto a three-by-five index card:

1. Makes me laugh.

2. Likes my children.

3. Won't abandon me if I get sick.

4. Can say *I love you.* Out loud.

5. Smells good.

I'm still secretly holding out for the two additional following requisites:

6. Tall enough for me to wear heels without viewing the top of his head.

7. Owns a lightweight Italian wool suit, crisply pressed white shirt, and platinum cufflinks.

I mean, these last two may make me appear incredibly shallow, but what the hell. A girl can still dream…can't she?

YES, MY HUSBAND IS REALLY DEAD (I'M NOT KIDDING)

Men (and women) who are divorced are notorious for saying stupid things to widows. At least this has been my experience. Especially if they harbor ill feelings toward their ex-spouses.

A number of years ago, I was out ballroom dancing with some friends. I went under duress and was not particularly happy to be there. And, as I danced with some mildly tolerable man from New Jersey, he asked me about my divorce. I told him I wasn't divorced and that my husband was dead. He burst out laughing and joyfully exclaimed, "I wish my ex were dead!"

Having been raised with rather good manners, I was silent until the music came to an end, dismissed myself graciously and told my friends there was no way in hell I was staying there with those losers. We then promptly headed off to a local cowboy bar, where we square-danced with a multitude of gay men and truck drivers, and drank too much cheap beer.

TELLING THE KIDS YOU'RE DATING

I'd like to talk with you about children...and dating. Not your own children going out on dates, but telling said children that you're dating other adults.

I've been dating for quite a while now, and I've dated a goodly number of divorced men. Of course, once you reach your forties, most available men are available because they are...divorced. If they're not divorced, they are generally eternal bachelors. Too busy taking all the available women out on their sailboats or to their ski chalets. Men like this don't generally constitute desirable long-term relationship material. In addition to eternal bachelors you may find a handful of widowers, but divorced men form the bulk of the dating pool.

Of course Drew died, which makes the situation very different from divorce. For both myself and my children. They miss their dad and I miss my husband. I wish I weren't dating, but I am.

Consequently, my children are along on the dating ride, as well. Full-time. And, by default, they often end up witnessing the fall-out from my romantic extravaganzas.

Although our children are very important, and we must be sensitive to their needs, we must remember that we are human beings as well, and as single parents, have not just the right but also the obligation to take care of ourselves. To tend to our own happiness. The analogy is putting on the oxygen mask when the plane loses cabin pressure: If you don't save yourself, you can't rescue your kids. The same goes for single parenting in the face of widowhood—you need to take care of yourself first so that you have the strength to take care of your offspring.

I've had talks with my children. I have let them know that they are my first priority, and that they are extraordinarily important. That they come before any man who may date me or be in my life. But eventually, I would like to have a man in my life who shares first place with my children. If push comes to shove, of course they're still going to come first...but my happiness is as important as theirs. And I have every right to have sex again in this lifetime. Thousands of times, in fact, if that's what I choose.

Parents who don't put their happiness right up there alongside their children's often find themselves in a situation where they end up becoming a big martyr, with a capital *M*. And then when the children go off to college—fly the coop—you are the one who's sitting at home with no career, perhaps no partner, no life. You have given all this up, thinking you're doing your children a big favor—doing what's necessary—when actually all you're doing is setting them up to feel guilty for the rest of their lives because their "poor mother" gave up all these important things just to focus on *them*.

This is not healthy for anyone involved. You get no life of your own, and your kids get served up a great big helping of guilt. No, no...no.

Recently, I dated a divorced gentleman who, after three years of being estranged from his wife and having a life of his own, still couldn't tell his child or talk to his ex about wanting to move on and be in a new relationship. He couldn't even broach the whole dating thing with them, just as a general topic of discussion.

He wanted to be dating me. He was, in fact, dating me. He wanted a "committed" relationship. But he was not ready to tell his child that he was dating, much less dating a specific person. Such as *me!*

I didn't need for my name or my children to be involved. I was not looking for an immediate *Brady Bunch* situation. But I do think that if a grown-up is widowed or divorced and still cannot, after a few years—even though they want to be dating—broach the subject with their offspring, that indicates a problem. They are clearly not ready to date.

Unfortunately, I learned this lesson the hard way.

So my point is, if you're widowed and have children…love them, respect them. Treat them with kindness and tenderness and sensitivity. But for God's sake, you are allowed to have sex. You are allowed to have a dating life. Do not feel guilty about being a healthy, normal, adult human being.

And do not, under any circumstances, allow your children to boss you around. At age nine, my youngest son, Cole, informed me, in no uncertain terms, that I was not allowed to have a relationship or marry anyone until he went off to college. By my calculations, that event was approximately a decade away. I told him I loved him more than life itself, but that he was not the boss of me. And that I was going to have a relationship if I found someone who loved us. All of us.

I then firmly, but lovingly, escorted him back to his bed. He hasn't tried pulling that one on me ever again.

DATING MISHAPS WITH KIDS

I'm here to give you the lowdown on dating with children in tow. I know you may be a bit worried when you first start dating. You might be apprehensive. You may be wondering:

What will my children think?

How will this affect them?

Am I going to ruin their little lives?

I can tell you, children are resilient. My children have lost their father. They are managing to thrive—not just survive, but thrive. A little dating "incident" here or there is virtually unavoidable, and doesn't compare to the death of a parent. So please, give yourself a break. Don't be so tough on yourself. No matter how responsible we attempt to be, none of us are perfect.

Stuff happens.

And no, you are not going to ruin your child's entire life because of a little dating faux pas.

First of all, be confident that if you are dating, and if you have children at home, and if, once in a while, a man actually has to come to your house, one or all of your children will, at some point, catch you doing something with him that you did not necessarily intend for them to see you doing.

The best-case scenario is that, perhaps, they see you smooching. Or canoodling on the couch. The worst-case scenario…well, you can imagine. Something involving partial or total nudity. Under covers. On top of covers. On the Oriental rug. Wherever. Unless you have a very low libido, or have a lot of money for decent hotels, it's going to happen.

OK, at this point, you may be thinking, *I would never do such a thing!*

Well, just wait until you haven't had sex in fourteen months, and then get back to me.

Of course, there is always the idea of expressing your affections in a motor vehicle, but this is just not something anyone over the age of twenty-three should be forced to do. Also, the authorities find it quite amusing to find two middle-aged lovers in a state of semi-undress in the front seat of a Volvo station wagon… plus you may end up listed in the police beat pages of your local newspaper.

Not that I would know anything about that sort of embarrassing predicament.

The thing is, those darned kids are going to catch you doing something, or suspect you are doing something (even if you aren't!) that you really didn't want them to know you were doing. Even though you used to do it with their father. And even though they have moved on with their lives—because they don't really want you moving on with yours. But you must. Because you aren't the one who is dead. You are very much alive.

Sometime when you are at home and in a state of partial undress (perhaps you have taken off your belt), or are just French-kissing a man, and the children are also at home—even if it is three a.m. and they have been fast asleep for five hours without stirring—at least one will wake up and walk in on you. This will happen at least once in your dating career. I assure you.

They are like little drug-sniffing dogs and they can smell

French-kissing or a square inch of naked flesh from a mile away.

I myself had a couple of unfortunate incidents featuring one of my sons. At the time he was maybe eight or nine. On one occasion, he walked into my living room, and caught me kissing someone I'd dated a handful of times. We were fully clothed—buttons buttoned, zippers zipped. We were totally respectable, but for the fact that we were lying on the floor in front of the fireplace with our lips touching.

The next morning, he, upon setting eyes on me, gave me his now-patented "death stare." I felt like a fifteen-year-old who had been caught by her father, having sex on the kitchen table. Yet here I was, a grown woman who had merely been kissing someone. Fully clothed, no less!

Child: "So, I saw you smooching with Enrique."

Me: "Yes."

Child: "So…what are his intentions? Is he planning on marrying you?"

Good God!

(The man in question was charming, cute, creatively talented, and brilliant. Of course, he also turned out to be on a daily regimen of a handful of various prescription medications to deal with a variety of mental disorders, which has turned out to be a theme in my dating life. Hopefully, it's not a reflection upon me. But, I'm still trying to figure that out. And that's a topic for another chapter.)

So, that was just a teeny-tiny incident.

Years later, in a different house, the same child—I repeat, the *same child*—climbs out of bed after having been seemingly comatose for hours, at a most inopportune moment. He must be a light sleeper. OK, this was a bad incident. I don't even like remembering it. I wasn't actually in the throes of intercourse, but I'll admit there was a smidgen of nudity involved. I'm not proud of it, but it happened. If it means anything to anyone, I have a divorced friend who once had a child walk in on him and his girlfriend as they were having sex. On the couch. Ouch. So, my incident, however much it distressed me, still seems mild in comparison.

I sent the boyfriend home, snuggled in bed with said child, and had a discussion about the incident immediately. Obviously, trying not only to temper my guilt but also to control the damage. The conversation went as well as could be expected.

I then waited a year and brought up the subject again, very gently, to see if he actually remembered. Unfortunately, he jumped right on it—he apparently remembered nearly everything. Now it's been years. But for one subsequent, roundabout mention of what had happened so long ago (when his response proved that he had definitely forgotten much of the details), I've never brought it up again. He has never brought it up again either. And I'm hoping it's buried deep in his psyche.

Granted, it may resurface again at some point, when he has a girlfriend or a wife, and there are certain things that give him a strange feeling that he just can't put into words. I mean, he could conceivably be broaching the subject with a health care professional at some point. God knows, we all have our issues from childhood. If we didn't, the therapists of the world would have nothing to do with their time. And they'd have no money with which to purchase vacation homes.

8

PARENTING

WEEKENDS

Is it Monday yet?

No one tells you that once you are alone with your children, you will dread the weekends. Where once the sound of the school bus approaching at three o'clock on a Friday afternoon signaled the beginning of a wonderful family weekend, it now signals the beginning of forty-eight-plus hours of unbearable time to think about the huge missing piece of your family puzzle.

I never realized that Drew's absence would not only ruin life in general for a long time, but weekends with my kids, in particular. While other families were looking forward to their "together" time…I was dreading it. No husband to run the kids to soccer games while I got a much-needed break from a long week of motherhood. No family breakfast at the local bagel place. No cartoons together on the couch. No shared coffee while the kids played outside on the swings. Nothing. Just a great big gaping hole in our hearts…where Drew should have been.

Eventually, the weekends got better. But, they're still a bit melancholy, even now. I sometimes sit alone in front of our fireplace on a Friday night, winding down from a long week, have my glass of wine, and I look into the flames and see the two of us, when we had tiny babies to care for, and treated ourselves to our Friday night ritual of a bottle of champagne and take-out food from our favorite Chinese restaurant, with some chocolate truffles for dessert. And I can still feel his arm around me, feel him snuggled up against me. As we silently prayed that the kids would sleep through just *one* Friday night.

Bliss is all around us. We often just don't see it while we are in the midst of it.

MOTHER'S DAY

Try not to cry when the kids attempt to make you breakfast and your husband isn't there to help them. Try not to cry when you realize that they don't have anyone to help them orchestrate the Mother's Day festivities.

Try not to cry when they give you the necklace made out of macaroni. And the pin that says *I love you Mommy*. Try not to feel guilty about how often you wonder why you were left all alone to raise three children. Even though you love them like mad, and they are the only piece of Drew that you have left, and they are the brightest light in your world.

FATHER'S DAY

Don't fall apart when the teacher sends home a note asking if you'd like your child to make the requisite Father's Day present for a grandfather, or uncle, or perhaps for you. Since there is no father available to gift. Remain calm when the teacher sends home a note asking if, perhaps, you'd prefer to just keep your child at home on the day the class will be making said Father's Day present...to avoid an unpleasant, emotionally difficult situation.

HEY! WHO ATE MY DAMNED SAUSAGE?!

This is a story about a sausage. One, single, crummy little sausage. Not even a really delectable, high-quality sausage, like you might get from the butcher counter at a place like Whole Foods. No. I am talking about your mass-produced, garden-variety sausage out of a box from the frozen food aisle at the local grocery store.

This tiny sausage unknowingly became a painful reminder of something missing in my life as of late. No, not sex. Consideration. That tiny sausage and the events of a certain Sunday morning in June were a reminder of the fact that I no longer have someone in my life (at least not on a consistent basis) who is concerned with my personal happiness. No one who is mature enough and who loves me enough to—*gasp!*—consider my needs.

Sometimes one of the worst things about being alone is having no one there who is thinking of your well-being. And when you are responsible for the care and feeding of three children, the fact that there is no one thinking of *your* happiness and *your* well-being becomes even more disheartening. A huge piece of the puzzle is missing. It doesn't matter how much you love yourself. It doesn't matter how many friends you have. How many family members who care about you. You still no longer have someone there on a daily basis. You no longer have that connectedness...that built in understanding...that unspoken promise that says something like, *If there is a sausage left, I will not eat it without asking if you'd like it. Or at least I'll offer to split it with you!*

It was a lovely Sunday morning. My children were relaxing. School had just ended and summer was officially upon us. I can tell you right now that I am not the type of mother who cooks her kids some labor-intensive breakfast every morning. But I do try, once in a while, to put forth the effort so they won't walk around someday proclaiming, *I don't ever remember my mother making us breakfast. I think I ate goldfish crackers every morning.* So I had offered to make one of their favorites: scrambled eggs, toast...and sausage.

Now my daughter, Olivia, was away and I had only two children with me. Boy children. I had my music on and was bopping around the kitchen, enjoying the summer sunshine, making scrambled eggs and toast...and heating up the frozen sausage. It smelled good. And it was going to taste good. School was out, and I was happy. Drew was still dead, but I was at the point where I could keep that in the recesses of my soul and once again find joy in the act of cooking breakfast for our kids on a Sunday morning...solo.

I was not weeping into the frying pan.

What happened next, however, changed my state of mind completely.

I went from happy to sad in the blink of an eye. Or rather, in the time it takes one twelve-year-old to eat a two-and-a-half-inch previously frozen sausage.

I picked out one of my favorite plates—one of the blue and white patterned porcelain ones that had been part of my grandmother's kitchen when I was a young girl. I treasure those plates. I put the sausage on the special plate.

I put the plate down onto the counter. It sat there happily waiting for me, while I had my back turned to it and was at the stove, preparing my perfectly yummy, gently scrambled eggs. I had made myself my favorite coffee in my new French press contraption. Sunshine was streaming through the windows.

As I said, life was not so bad.

Until I turned around and I saw my paternal grandmother's blue and white kitchen plate, somehow, suddenly, naked. There was no sausage. I glanced around the kitchen. Where was my damned sausage? For a brief moment in time, I even wondered to myself if I had eaten it and somehow forgotten. But, no, that wasn't it. I knew I was not going out of my mind. Not on this particular morning, at least. It was at that moment that my then nine-year-old son, Cole, came strolling through the kitchen. I stopped him in his tracks: "Did you eat my sausage?"

No, he hadn't eaten my sausage. "Well, someone ate my sausage! It was sitting right here, on this plate. Now it's *not* on this plate! What the heck happened to my sausage?"

I was clearly losing it and Cole, being the intelligent and

sensitive child that he is, could sense that his mother was about to blow a fuse.

"Did your brother eat my sausage? Where is he?!"

As I stood in my kitchen, transforming from Ms. Perfect Mommy into some vision from Dante's *Inferno*, I heard Cole out in the driveway: "*Holden!* Did you eat Mom's sausage?"

My twelve-year-old came into the kitchen, his usual easygoing self. "Oh…I didn't know that was your sausage. I just saw it on the plate. I thought no one was going to eat it. So I ate it."

OK. This made perfect sense to a twelve-year-old. Lonely looking sausage. Prepubescent stomach sends direct order to eat loner sausage. Brain is not connected to stomach. It made no matter that he had already consumed eight of the ten sausages I had cooked that morning. Cooked? Who am I kidding? We are talking about those frozen things that are already cooked. This is not gourmet fare, as I already mentioned. Which only made the loss of my one crappy, cheap little sausage treat all the more poignantly painful.

Was I not worthy of one crappy, cheap, frozen sausage?

I recall babbling something about *consideration,* and something else about singular sausages not generally being found hanging out on a spanking-clean plate unless it was meant for someone's breakfast.

Then I just lost it. The next thing I remember was climbing the stairs to my bedroom, feeling as if I had just been newly widowed. I collapsed onto my bed and just sobbed. And mumbled obscenities into my pillow for a good fifteen minutes, or possibly even longer. I sobbed and swore until nothing else was left to come out. It was a familiar laundry list:

- *I am so fucking tired of being all alone.*

- *I am so fucking tired of taking care of everything and everyone all by myself.*

- *I am so fucking tired of having no one who is here for me.*

And, a new one to add to the list:

- *I am so fucking tired of no one caring about my happiness. All I wanted was that one damned sausage!*

OK. That last one does sound a lot funnier in hindsight. But, the message is still the same. It's lonely at the top…when you're alone. Sometimes you just want someone there to save a sausage for you.

SPEED-GRIEVING

"Mommy, can we stop being sad now?"

Children don't have much tolerance for grieving. Or crying. They don't want to see their remaining parent curled up in a ball on her bed, with swollen eyes and a red nose. They want you to move on, dammit!

Well, at least one of my children did. He told it like it was.

Drew was in the film business, and he taught me about something called *magic hour*. It's a brief, fleeting time, right before the sun dips down below the horizon. A string of moments when everything and everyone appears more perfect than they do in the harsh light of day. I thought it was the perfect description and, as an artist, I too loved and appreciated the beauty of those last, golden rays of the sun—those perfect, if fleeting, moments.

On the day my husband died, there was a magic hour...but I didn't notice. Everything went dark on that bright winter's day long before the sun set in the December sky. And it remained dark until forty-eight hours later, when Holden, then seven, came into our bedroom. He quietly approached me as I lay in our bed, crying silent tears that wouldn't stop flowing, and said quite bluntly, "Mommy, can we stop being sad now?"

And although his tiny voice lilted upward towards the sentence's end, to suggest a question, as the words streamed from his mouth...it was clearly more a statement of desire, or strongly felt suggestion, than a question.

It had been two days since his daddy's death, and he was ready to get back to life as usual, and move on. His young, fragile heart couldn't process the permanent absence of his father but, even more, it couldn't process having his previously energetic and optimistic mother incapacitated by grief.

That was a defining moment.

That was when I knew I was going to have to find a way to get through the darkness...because my children needed me to be their sunlight. Had I not had children, I would have undoubtedly been in that bed, curled up, drowning in my own tears, for many more months to come.

This is both the blessing and the curse of grieving the loss of your husband, and your children's father, while living in the same house with these children. You must grieve, you cannot push your grief away, because it will resurface with a fury and force worse than anything you can imagine. There is no such thing as speed-grieving, but you have to find a way to cry your own tears, help your children to heal from their own very different loss, while still getting up and seeing clearly enough to make them French toast every morning. And if you do it wrong, if you don't do it by your own rules, you'll pay for it later.

And it won't be pretty.

I thank my children and their cherubic little faces, whether tear-stained, giggling, or smiling, for giving me the strength to pull myself up out of the depths of overwhelming despair. They gave me a reason to live, to smile, to laugh, and to wake up every day. Until I was able to do it just for myself once again. Just for the love of things like magic hour…and the appreciation of life, itself.

KARATE MAKES ME CRY

So does shoe shopping…and school plays, parent-teacher conferences, and Little League games.

After Drew had died, it seemed every "normal" thing I had to do with our children made me cry. Every time I'd witness a father sitting happily by, watching his son or daughter doing some normal kid thing, and probably taking those times together for granted, it made my heart ache just a little more deeply. What made it even more unbearable was that my Holden was a gabber. He loved to tell anyone who would listen that his daddy had died. Not only was I crying at his karate meets and at the shoe stores, but he had other parents weeping…everywhere.

I vividly recall once roaming the aisles of a family clothing store in our little town, not too many weeks after the funeral, searching for new sneakers for Holden, when I suddenly realized he had gone astray. As I walked toward the next aisle and rounded the corner, I heard his little voice. And there he was, standing in front of some other mother, apparently regaling her with the tale of his loss. "Do you know my dad died?" was one of his best opening lines. And I'd generally find his adult victims standing speechless, with glassy eyes, or, if he was really on a roll, tears silently cascading down their cheeks.

Another time, we were taking a hiatus with my mother, down on Cape Cod, our old family vacation stomping grounds. As we stood on the fish pier with all three children one day, waiting to view the arrival and unloading of the fishermen's morning catch, Holden struck up a conversation with the family milling about in front of us. After first shocking the father with his fatherlessness, Holden moved on to a more intimate and detailed conversation with the man's daughter, who appeared to be close to his own age. As we hovered far enough behind to provide breathing room for their budding friendship, but still within listening distance, we were privy to the following exchange:

> *Holden:* "Well, you know, my Mom's a widow. That's what she is. A widow. That's when your husband dies. And he did. He just died. He just died of cancer. Yup, he just *died* of cancer."

> *Girl:* "Yeah. I have two grandmas, and one of them died of cancer. Right on my couch!"

Mind you, these were tiny people…maybe eight years old. They sounded like a couple of twenty-five-year-olds. I almost expected the next words I'd hear from their mouths to be details about his father's chemotherapy (from Holden), and a great big, *Can you believe it?? Right on our fucking couch!* (from his new acquaintance).

Once again, my heart broke—yet at the same time, I found myself wanting to laugh. In fact, I'm pretty sure, if memory serves, that I was smiling through my tears.

This seems to happen quite often when you are first widowed, and have children.

It still happens.

In the nine years since his death, I've wept my way through school plays, elementary, middle, and high school graduations, field trips, parent-teacher conferences, premiers of a large number of Disney and Pixar movies (Drew was a film guy, remember?), and special education meetings. And if I wasn't weeping *during* those events, I snuck into a bathroom to do it, or saved it up for the car ride home. Or waited until I was tucked safely back in my bed later that night, where no one could notice the telltale bits of tissue lint adorning my eyelashes.

At the time, Holden's outspoken way of sharing his grief made my heart break in a way I never thought possible. For him, for our newly reduced family of four, and for me. Looking back, I can see how necessary and healthy it was for him. And although it still breaks my heart, it also makes me smile. Partly because I know it would have made Drew smile. A *that's my boy!* brand of smile.

PIECES OF DREW

It's both heartwarming and heartbreaking to see traits of Drew show up in our children as they have grown, changed, and matured in the years since his death.

The first time I glanced out at Cole, standing in the field at his first Little League game, I had to catch my breath. There he was, his little second-grade self, standing in the midst of a bunch of eager-beaver baseball-playing kids with dedicated eager-beaver baseball-loving fathers on the sidelines—his hips askew, his little-boy-size hands stuffed partially into his pockets. Too cool to look too terribly interested in what he was doing.

He was a tiny carbon copy of his father. In fact, I have photos of Drew in that exact pose in college, in his twenties, in his thirties. Probably right up to his death at age forty-two. Drew wasn't alive long enough to make much of a visual impact upon Cole, who had just turned four when he died.

So, as with his movie star good looks and his huge, ultra-bright smile, I can only blame my youngest child's stance, and his coolness, on genetics.

There's another thing about my youngest child that I find fascinating: he has always been in love with the Beatles. Truthfully, like the baseball field stance, it freaks me out a bit.

I never listened to the Beatles—or even had an album, eight-track, tape, or CD of their music in my hands—until I met Drew. He loved the Beatles. When John Lennon died, during our college years, he was in mourning. In fact, I don't think he ever really got over it. He had grown up with a house full of seven older brothers and sisters in the 1960s, and they provided a first class ticket to the Beatles' invasion of the American music scene. Meanwhile, I was the oldest child while growing up, and missed out on the entire thing. So any predetermined Beatlemania seems to have come from Drew.

Can a child be drawn to certain bands genetically?

Then there's Olivia, our oldest. A few years into our fatherless familyhood, I stumbled upon a notebook that had been pulled from a drawer. As I slowly turned the pages, my heart nearly stopped. My eyes alighted on a sprinkling of doodles…just like the ones Drew had drawn when I knew him in college. Just like the ones he would scribble while talking on the phone or working on a home repair shopping list before a trip to Home Depot. He was an artist, and his doodles adorned the corners of random pieces of paper, grocery lists, and maps of vacation destinations. Sometimes I'd find them on napkins. Or tax documents.

Doodlers have their own style. My doodles, for instance, looked nothing like Drew's.

It obviously wasn't an old college notebook of his, although we did have a couple of those, stored. But Drew hadn't been around for years and we'd already moved to Maine, which had involved much sorting and tossing out. Seeing his doodles made my eyes well up with tears. For a split second, I thought he was still alive. Living with us in the same house. The mind plays tricks on us, and we sometimes get a glimpse into the reality that the concept of "time" is merely a human invention.

They turned out to be Olivia's doodles. She had inherited not only his thick, dark, wavy hair, chocolaty brown eyes, and warm, dazzling smile…but his doodling style, as well.

The genetic inheritance of Holden, our middle child, lies less in the physical realm than his brother's and sister's. But Holden's sensitivity, good manners, graciousness, and go-with-the-flow, laid back, gentle, and caring nature remind me of Drew each day.

Just so you don't think Drew was without fault, or that our marriage was without any negative tension, I should mention that our children have also inherited some of the things about him that used to drive me to distraction. His ability to be a bit *too* relaxed and laid back—to fall asleep in the midst of a five-alarm discussion, or watch movies for seven consecutive hours while the sun shone outside on a lovely Saturday afternoon. Not to mention an inclination to avoid all forms of strenuous exercise. But it's still a reminder of him. And I always make it a point to tell the children about the things I see in them that remind me of their dad. The special and unique things that make them his children.

THE GREAT HOLDINI

Holden was physically challenging as a small child. So much so that Drew dubbed him The Great Holdini. It was the perfect nickname, since Holden was indeed not unlike Harry Houdini, the master of the great escape. That child could escape from any place and any thing. Holden climbed out of windows, scaled white picket fences, and moved faster than a hamster in a Habitrail.

"Hello, Mrs. Amorello? Do you know your toddler is climbing out of your second story window onto your roof?"

Once, a few days after bringing the newborn Cole home from the hospital, I was hiding out in our upstairs bedroom, performing my motherly breastfeeding duties. I was understandably exhausted, given that shortly after having given birth I returned home to a two-year-old and his five-year-old sister. It was late afternoon on a day in mid-October, and my mother was in the kitchen preparing dinner, while Drew was ostensibly entertaining our other two offspring in the den. In actuality, I imagine he was watching *This Old House*. So, while I was in my peaceful, darkened bedroom, there were two adults downstairs whose main responsibility was to keep an eye on two children. That's one adult per child, not an impossible task.

Suddenly, I heard the muffled sounds of a commotion downstairs. Then voices called up the stairwell, asking whether I had seen Holden. A moment later, panicked, they said to call 911— Holden had disappeared. I thought I was in some sort of bad movie. There I was, in the trance of new-motherhood, with udderlike, uncomfortable breasts and leaking nipples, merely wishing for a few hours of sleep and, perhaps, a bottle of baby formula to administer to the newest addition to our family, when I found myself thrust into an episode of *Columbo*.

In addition to being a bit pissed-off, and honestly wondering how the hell two adults could have managed to allow my two-year-old to escape while I was dealing with a newborn, my hormonal levels had yet to return to anything close to normal. The news that my toddler was missing in action sent me into a tailspin.

Drew and my mother ran outside to start the frantic search while I called the police. I was balancing Cole in one arm as I spoke into the receiver, my voice cracking and tears running down my cheeks as I tried to get the words out.

As the officer took the information, I peered through the window of our den, praying I'd catch a glimpse of Holden climbing over a neighbor's fence. The sun was setting as cruisers, policemen, family, and neighbors scoured the streets.

Four or five police cars with a pair of officers each were dispatched to locate him. But in the end, they weren't the ones to do it. The little old lady who lived diagonally across the street, and spoke only her native Italian, ended up being the one to spot him. He was, apparently, investigating her back yard, which housed vegetable gardens and live chickens. He had found a pre-Halloween pumpkin that caught his attention and had decided her yard was more fun than being confined to a house with a crying newborn baby brother.

Another of my favorite memories I keep filed away under "Holden's Shenanigans" involves, once again, my nursing his baby brother. Drew would head off to work and I, of course, would be left at home with my three charges.

Even though it was December, Holden needed his exercise, and a day with no outdoor playtime was a day when we didn't look forward to trying to get him to go to sleep that night. Because it just wasn't going to happen.

I started off cleverly thinking that if I nursed his little brother while sitting at our dining room table, I'd have the perfect place to keep an eye on Holden as he played outside. Our house was circa 1870, and there was a door in our dining room that led directly to a small porch, with the driveway and yard beyond it. Our yard was 85 percent fenced in, and the remaining 15 percent of the perimeter was dense shrubbery and a small area that abutted a rather steep incline, spotted with trees and rocks. So I felt confident that, should he make a run for it, I was close enough to the door to plunk two-month-old Cole down in his baby carrier and chase down his older brother, who had just turned three.

Wrong. This was not a good plan, as I quickly found out. With just that small head start, Holden could outrun me—even in his snowsuit. Clearly, the dining room was not close enough. Holden was plowing his way through the boxwood hedge into the neighbor's yard before I could turn the doorknob and say, "Please God, let me survive this child's childhood."

With Plan A an obvious failure, I was forced to come up with a Plan B. So, instead of sitting in my warm dining room, I spent a good chunk of the winter in my parka, wedged in the driver's seat of our small blue Chrysler Neon as my infant son suckled from my maternal bosom. Holden could run like a free-range chicken around the yard, and I'd be only a car door away from grabbing him before he scaled our fence or wormed his way through the boxwood hedge.

Given his Great Holdini track record, I never would have believed the day would come when I would be forced to pry him from his bed after fourteen hours' sleep—but being sixteen will do that.

To quote one of Holden's favorite sayings, "Ahhh yes. Good times. Good times." And, actually, in spite of the exhaustion, looking back into the rearview mirror of my life, they were, indeed.

"IS THAT A NIGHTGOWN?"

Holden also loves to give fashion advice. He has always had an amazing ability to compliment a woman while simultaneously stabbing her in the back.

"I love those shoes." (Silent pause.) "It's too bad you didn't have the right color dress to match."

His commentary has caused many people much laughter over the years. He's always been this way. Cute, charming, and deadly.

My favorite is when he looks at me as I am dressing to leave the house for a date. The last time he did this, I was getting ready for a dinner date, throwing on different outfits, not particularly pleased with any one of them. Having finally settled on a knee-length, floral print rayon dress that I thought at least enhanced my cleavage, I was ready to go. Holden, thirteen at the time, stood in my bedroom doorway, looking at me…expressionless.

Me: "Well? What do you think?"

Holden: "Is that a nightgown?"

I had just spent half an hour, trying to put together the right outfit. One comment from him was all it took. I looked at myself in the mirror, took off the dress, and started a new pile for the Goodwill.

He may be deadly, but he is almost always right.

SPECIAL ED IS NOT FOR SISSIES

Dealing with your husband's death is one thing. Dealing with your grieving children is another. But dealing with the reality that he died and left you to raise children who have inherited some of his "quirky" genes is just too much to handle some days.

Drew's family history included a liberal sprinkling of people with some brand of dyslexia. Of course, they're all doing quite marvelously as adults and, undoubtedly, making more money than I currently am—but still, they've had their educational challenges. Drew wasn't ever diagnosed himself, but looking back, he did exhibit some classic symptoms, although mild. It seems to run in the XY chromosomal combination more than in the XX. Which is probably how our daughter managed to avoid it, while our sons have both had learning challenges.

Around the same time that we found out about his incurable pancreatic cancer, we were also getting the first real signs that our older son was, perhaps, not completely on track developmentally with most of the other children at the preschool he attended a couple of times a week. And so, not long after Drew's death, I found myself bound for North Carolina, flying with seven-year-old Holden for the purpose of an educational assessment with a very well-known specialist. Continuing a process that we'd begun while he still had a father.

I still deal with the boys' issues and have struggled to help them with their struggles over the years. Fortunately (or unfortunately, depending upon how you look at it), I've had the money to pay for educational attorneys, tutors, and, during one three-month stretch of particular desperation, a private school. This is only due to the fact that (drum roll please) Drew had what would be considered by some to be rather generous life insurance.

I often look upward toward the heavens and say, with a good dose of the kind of sarcasm I know Drew would have appreciated, *Thank you so much for leaving me here to deal with all of this all alone. And on top of that, they're your genes!*

Once again, single parenting and grief is a tough combination.

If you have never had the pleasure of dealing with this country's public school system, and our special education system, in particular, then consider yourself blessed. It doesn't seem to matter what state you're in or what town you're in (although some school systems do seem easier to deal with than others), it's akin to navigating a minefield. The very people who are supposed to be there to help your child when he or she is struggling are, all too often, the same people who appear to wish to do everything in their power to take away the services guaranteed by hard-fought-for laws, or to grant your struggling and frustrated child the minimal amount of assistance possible.

Of course, there are good apples in with the rotten ones. But in my own experience, and in the experience of many other mothers I know, many of those employed under the auspices of special education are, apparently, Satan's disciples. Hell-bent on seeing that your wonderful child, who perhaps is not of the educational "cookie cutter" variety, suffers unnecessarily.

I recall once attending a meeting at the middle school for the training of "parent volunteers." Don't ask me how I ended up there, but I'm sure it was during a period when my youngest child was in the throes of elementary-school-special-education torment, and I felt the need to compensate for his heartache by offering myself up for as many field trips as possible, to comfort and soothe his wounded little soul.

One of the training topics was how to treat children who are "different," in case you are volunteering for little Johnny's field trip and suddenly find yourself in the presence of a child with a learning disability. Of course, they lumped the kids with autism right in there with the children, like my son, with a reading delay. They didn't go into much differentiation.

As I sat at the cafeteria table along with maybe a dozen or so other parents, I realized that I was probably the only one there who actually had any real-life experience with kids requiring special services—or with the special education system itself. This became especially clear when a mother raised her hand and asked for more detail about how to treat "these special ed kids." The training "leader" explained about how "special" these special ed kids were. And then went on to explain the rudimentaries of "the system" and the particulars of the school administrators and educational staff who are part of the planning and delivery of a child's I.E.P. (individual education program).

I nearly laughed out loud as this syrupy sweet woman, who looked not unlike Mrs. Cleaver (the Beaver's mother) in pedal pushers and a 1950s style top, exclaimed with unbridled excitement, "It's just wonderful. It's amazing. They're miracle workers!"

I had recently sat through a year's worth of special education meetings for my youngest son, at tables occupied by not only an entire platoon of school authorities and teachers but also an educational attorney's assistant, a therapist, and an educational tutor funded by Drew's life insurance money—money that could have been better used to send one of our children to college.

So I had to restrain myself to keep from bursting into laughter. That or grabbing her by the pearl buttons on her pale pink twinset and giving her a piece of my maternal mind.

As a single mother, I was fairly certain that, although the school administration pretended to sympathize with the fact that my children were rather recently left fatherless, I didn't receive quite the same treatment that women received if they showed up with their husband, or ex-husband, in tow. Anyone with a penis would do—at least that's what I'd heard through the parental grapevine.

Sadly, I couldn't get Drew to come back from the grave to help out, and in spite of my continued dating efforts, couldn't find a man to fill this position. I did consider hiring a special education gigolo at more than one juncture.

Special education laws are diabolical and ever-changing, and even when you have two parents fighting for a child's right to an appropriately tweaked education, it's tough to keep up with the legal mumbo-jumbo and get what you need. The entire process is exhausting, and all too often becomes a full-time job that a grief-stricken parent simply doesn't have the emotional strength to deal with. I've often found it easier to pay a tutor than to deal with the tears, stress, and emotional havoc special ed hath wreaked upon our entire little family in the years since Drew's death.

Miracle workers, indeed. The only miracle is that both of my sons are still in possession of any of their self-esteem. And that, after all of this, I have any of Drew's life insurance money left for college.

I ADMIT IT...I LOVE BOYS

If you've read the preceding chapter, you may be saying, *duh* right now. But I'm not talking men here. I'm talking men in the making. Boys. I love listening to them talk. I love hearing them belly laughing down the hall and plotting and planning and scheming.

This surprises me more than anyone. And there's no longer much that surprises me.

I gave birth to two boy children, Holden and Cole, whom I adore. I adore their older sister, Olivia, as well. In fact, she was the first object of my maternal affection, and I was thrilled to have given birth to a creature I could clothe in cute little things. My mother bought her French pajamas in the finest and most delicate of cottons. She was a girl! Sugar and spice and everything nice.

When I was pregnant the second time, Olivia was two years old and certain that she was going to get a little sister. She had me convinced of this. However, she was apparently not blessed with psychic capabilities, because the child that came out of my body had a penis. And as they handed me this new, pink, squirmy bundle of joy, I cried. Not because I was disappointed, but because I could not believe the feeling of joy that overcame me. I recall lying there, cradling my new baby boy, gushing, "I just never thought I'd be so happy to have a boy!"

Then, it happened *again*, two years and ten months later. Another bungled prediction. Another boy.

Boys are a lot of work, but I am finally reaping the benefits as I watch them becoming fully formed human beings—not just Lego-building, Tonka-truck-smashing creatures with their hands constantly in their training pants.

These are the days I treasure, because I know so well they will not last forever.

Do you know what one of my favorite things is? I can't believe it myself. Really. I love to drive a car full of boys somewhere. Anywhere. I sit there quietly and just listen. I listen to their stories and their teasing and their goofy jokes and their laughter. I listen to them as they attempt to correct and impress one another. And strut their stuff.

Sometimes I get goose bumps. And I'm not sure why. I just find it so wonderful. Every car ride is like that movie *Stand by Me*.

So when they want to go skateboarding an hour from home with a few friends, and they plead, *Mom, will you drive us?* I almost always say yes. And their friends' mothers often think I have lost my mind. But I tell them I love to drive them. It's like being in a car with a bunch of funny, adorable aliens.

I find them magical. Maybe it's because they're foreign territory. My daughter is magical, and mothers and daughters share a bond that goes beyond the word *magical*. But I know how that bond works. I am a daughter. I have a mother. But this mother-son thing is all new to me.

So, yes, although I'm sure I would have loved three girls, I'm happy beyond measure that we were blessed with a few more Y chromosomes. Even if every once in a while I trip over a snake, snail, or puppy-dog tail.

Photographic Evidence

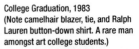

College Graduation, 1983
(Note camelhair blazer, tie, and Ralph Lauren button-down shirt. A rare man amongst art college students.)

Sandi & Drew, college, summer of 1982
(Newly in love…and thankfully clueless as to what the future had in store.)

Wedding bliss, 1988
DeCordova Museum, Lincoln, MA

Drew, film job, 1989
(Attempting to look very
mysterious & rugged.)

Honeymoon in Maine, autumn of 1988
(Never in my wildest imagination did I think I'd
be living here one day. Never mind without him!)

Two kids later and still in love, 1996 (And still goofy.)

Superdad, 1996
Drew, Olivia, and Holden

Cole's Homecoming, 1998
(Child #3: Let the games begin!)

Christmastime, 1999
(Olivia is still trying to recover from those bangs.)

Drew & Sandi, autumn of 2000
(Does this man look terminally ill?)

Drew & Cole, autumn 2000

Halloween 2000
("Woody" from Toy Story surely never
looked this hot.)

The "boys"—Drew, Holden, and Cole, 2001

Grammi Louise and kids,
Cape Cod, 2004

Drew—master robot designer
and birthday party organizer
extraordinaire, 2001
(Holden's 6th Birthday)

Moving Day, July 2005
Our new life begins

Cole at one of our favorite new
beaches, Maine, 2006

Holden's 8th Grade graduation, 2011

Holden's 16th Birthday, 2011
(And Cole ruins yet another perfect
family photo. Oh Cole!)

The Irreverent Widow, 2011
Wearing black...but smiling!
(The dark days are over.)

9

DATING AND SEX — INTERMEDIATE

THE FIRST KISS

Adolescence revisited

I WAS NERVOUS about kissing someone again. Never mind that I had approximately twenty-eight years of kissing experience under my belt. The truth was, the more time went by, the more insecure I became. I knew in my heart that it was like riding a bike—it all would come back to me once I did it. But, the thought of "doing it" became more and more distressing as the days, weeks, and months ticked by.

At one point, I knew the dreaded (but also much anticipated) first kiss was imminent, and my stomach was in the proverbial knot.

I find it hard to admit to this, being a forty-something woman and not a fourteen-year-old, but at one point I actually practiced kissing. Yes. I practiced on oranges and peaches and even the fleshy part on the side of my hand…below my thumb. I thought of drawing a pair of lips in Sharpie marker to make it seem more real, but I was afraid the cashier at the local wine shop might notice it the next time I went in to purchase some cabernet.

The first kiss went surprisingly well. Luckily, he was a great kisser.

Not every man is, however. Now I am a great kisser. I'm not bragging, I'm merely relaying the consistent feedback I've been given over the years. And I'm sorry, but it's not a subjective thing. You either are or you aren't. There's no in-between.

Drew was a wonderful kisser. We could kiss for hours on end. And when he kissed me, my knees went weak and my head started spinning. I was transported into another dimension. That's what kissing is supposed to be all about. You are supposed to melt. Into a puddle. Even after twenty years. Yes, OK, my expectations are a bit high. That's what happens when you're used to gold-medal kissing. I am not settling for any bronze medalists at this point in my life. And I certainly don't want any semi-finalists or guys who couldn't even make the team.

Now, I have dated quite a bit since my second "first kiss." I have done my share of investigative kissing, and let me tell you, there are men who apparently have never been set straight. How could a man have been married for eight or ten or thirteen years, and not know how to kiss a woman properly? I've pondered this for a long time and, after encountering a disconcerting number of kissing-challenged men, have come to the conclusion that their wives didn't know how to kiss, either. Or their wives never kissed a good kisser when they learned how to kiss.

My theory is that being a good kisser hinges upon the quality of the kissing with the first person you kiss. If he or she is good then you learn the correct way. If he or she is mediocre or heaven forbid, bad, then you go through life disappointing everyone.

I have dealt with wet, slobbery kissers, dry kissers, and kissers whose tongue appeared to not in any way be connected to the control center of their brain. I kissed a man whose tense little tongue darted nervously in and out of my mouth. Like some sort of lizard tongue or a frog when it's trying to catch a fly. In out, in out.

It was very annoying and decidedly not sensual. I felt as if I were being attacked by the little slippery pimento inside a stuffed cocktail olive.

It was not difficult to jump to the conclusion that his lovemaking would be an expanded version of this same guerilla warfare technique, so I decided it would be less painful to end it at the kissing stage, rather than endure the perils of what might transpire in bed some day, down the road: in-out-in-out-in-out-in-out-in-out-in-out...and...snore.

I have also kissed men whose tongues were neither darting nor prodding, but were, worse still, nowhere to be found. The tongue should always be right there, in position—ready for engagement. I kissed one particular man whose tongue was never around. Where had it disappeared to, I thought? Then there is the opposite problem, wherein the man's tongue can easily be located, and it is somewhere down around your tonsils.

I haven't had tonsils since the age of five, so my adenoids are the organs in greatest danger.

And kissing is not something you can teach someone very easily, especially after the age of thirty. I mean, you might think you have fixed the problem; he may seem to be reformed. But a few hours or days later, his old, bad habits will resurface. He will slobber again. Or worse.

Of course, once I got that first kiss over with, it was like someone had reignited my pilot light. I couldn't stop thinking about kissing.

ADVENTURES IN KISSING

A couple of months into my fledgling dating career, I accepted a dinner date with a man whom I admittedly wasn't too sure about. I had met him on Match.com, and due to the quality of his photographs (tiny, grainy), it was hard to ascertain how attracted I actually felt to him. At least on the physical level. On what turned out to be our only real "date," we went to a lovely restaurant in Providence, Rhode Island, a full hour from my house, and had a lovely dinner. But rather than being entranced with things like his smile, or the delectability of the port wine reduction that glazed my pork tenderloin, my mind was occupied with one thought, and one thought alone:

Do I want to kiss you?

I am certain he was blathering on with all manner of fascinating dinner conversation, but as I looked across the table, feigning interest in current events and talk of children's shenanigans, all I was thinking about was how much time I had left until I would come face-to-face with the kissing decision. Tick-tock. Tick-tock.

The clock was going to strike twelve momentarily. And I was feeling not unlike Cinderella at the ball.

Although, for me, morphing into a pumpkin at midnight might have been a pleasing option.

Dinner seemed over all too soon, and as my date walked beside me down the city sidewalk, awash in the harsh glare of the street-lights, an undercurrent of nervousness rose in me. I couldn't find my car!

We decided he would give me a ride back to my car—partly because it was raining, but mostly due to the fact that I had, apparently, misplaced my own vehicle in a city I wasn't familiar with. As we climbed into his front seat, I thanked him for an enjoyable evening and thought about whether I should (a) give him a kiss on the cheek or (b) give him a quick peck on the lips. These were the only two options I was considering.

I remember thinking that if I could manage to get into my own car and on the road home in a time-efficient manner, it might still be early enough to make a phone call. (See "Dr. Tall, Dark and Naughty" later in this chapter; in the world of dating, the man you've just had an awkward dinner with can make the last guy look a whole lot better.)

So that was what was running through my brain as we searched for my lost car—whether or not the barely noticeable kiss should be on the cheek or the mouth. But the next thing I remember, it was two hours later and my lips were pleasantly numb. I had, in fact, given him one little kiss. One. And suddenly, boom! There I was, on a cold, rainy night in November, making out in his little German sports car, under a streetlight in downtown Providence.

I was like a woman possessed. Although he was not my dream date, he was a great kisser, and every time I opened my eyes, he looked more and more attractive. It's amazing what an effect passionate kissing can have on one's vision, after a lengthy drought. At one point, I recall hearing the familiar ring of my cell phone emanating from my purse as my sister-in-law, who was babysitting the kids, called in vain, probably wondering where I was at one a.m., and whether my date had abducted me.

I ignored the calls. I couldn't help myself. Like a cocaine addict who needed just one more line, I couldn't stop. Who cared if Drew's sister had to go to work in seven hours? I was being kissed by someone who knew how to kiss—finally! And I was damned if anyone was going to stop me.

I finally listened to my voicemail messages and reluctantly (and a bit embarrassingly) called back to say I was alive and had not been taken hostage by my dinner date. And as I began the hour-long journey home, with lips that were tingling, a head that was spinning, and a poor, benevolent sister-in-law who undoubtedly wanted to put me in "bad mommy jail," I realized that I didn't care what happened to me when I returned home. The crime was worth the punishment.

I did eventually meet up with this gentleman again. And I did sleep with him. Once. I imagined if the kissing was *that* good, the sex couldn't be all that bad, either. And I was right, it was actually quite wonderful. But although he was a lovely person and had good intentions, it just wasn't the level of total attraction I was searching for. And really, the kissing thing was all that mattered. I wanted to be reassured that there were men out there who were gold-medal quality. Even if I wasn't ready for much more than that quite yet.

I felt alive again.

ACTIVE WITHIN ONE HOUR

The pitfalls of Internet dating

When you have just returned from a seemingly-perfect romantic weekend with the man you've been dating for a couple of months, the last thing you want to see is that cute little status message on his Match.com profile page that cheerfully announces "Active within one hour." This, for those unfamiliar with Internet dating, means that the man who brought you coffee in bed just this morning has been unable to keep his busy little hands off his Match.com account since you left him. Romantic weekend be damned.

Those four little words, innocent on their own but deadly when formed into a phrase, are at the heart of the real problem with Internet dating. You are under a microscope.

In real-life dating, things like this just don't happen. In real life, you have privacy. Unless the man you're dating is loony tunes and has installed nanny-cams in the draperies, and hidden microphones in your houseplants while you were cooking dinner and he was supposed to be fixing your bathroom faucet, you do not, for the most part, need to be concerned about anyone knowing your business.

When you go the Internet dating route, however, it's an entirely different ballgame. You really have no secrets. At least not where your dating communications (and innocent, or possibly not so innocent flirtations) that float through the ether may be concerned.

In real life, you could, realistically, have a dinner date with a nice-enough gentleman, stop at the local grocery store on the way home to pick up a half-pound of American cheese for your thirteen-year-old son, and enjoy a flirtatious exchange with the cute guy with the Brad Pitt grin standing beside you at the deli counter. And your aforementioned dinner date, to whom you might be attracted but to whom you have no commitment, has no way of being privy to this innocent exchange. He knows nothing about Mr. Deli Counter. Nor should he.

In the twisted world of Match.com dating, however, you can have a pleasant—if not head-over-heels-in-love—dinner date, and later return home to find an email from a potential new suitor waiting in your in-box. If you answer (or merely view!) said email, you'll be technologically branded as being "active within one hour." Or within twenty-four hours, three days, five days, three weeks, etc. Whether you've been initiating correspondence, reading or responding to correspondence, or merely browsing the candy store, there is no way of hiding it from anyone.

The "active within" stamp is the scarlet letter of modern times. A virtual big red *A*—a symbol of your potential Internet dating sins.

This is a painful and unnecessary component of Match.com's dating process. I have never aspired to be a spy. And furthermore, I've never aspired to date one. I usually trust people. Perhaps there is a way to turn this feature off. If so, please enlighten me, because I've never succeeded in finding it.

Even if you are not the type of person who would ever spy on a man, the mere knowledge that checking this status is so easy makes it difficult for even the most trusting of women to abstain. I am not too ashamed to admit that I have found myself on both sides of this Internet dating coin. I've been both spy and spyee.

Either way, it's not a pretty picture.

Of course, if you are the one checking up on the man with whom you just had a fabulously romantic third date, and by whom you were just passionately kissed for fifty-five minutes, and then you immediately go home and log onto Match.com to see if he is a weasel, when you confront him with his weaslehood, he can come back at you with the standard *Well, what were* you *doing on there?!*

I've only been in a couple of situations with men like this. Both appeared to be smitten with me but, as I suspected, incapable of even a single day's worth of Internet dating commitment, and were "active" within a mere hour…or twenty-four. Needless to say, although this computer-spawned data did provide me with insight into their respective characters, I still needed them to commit "real life" dating atrocities in order to finally say good-bye to their sorry behinds. Like being spotted out in public making googly eyes across the table at another woman while on a lunch date. Or taking my friend's brother's ex-fiancée on a skiing vacation, while claiming to be working. That sort of stuff.

The entire situation is simply unhealthy. And unnatural.

In my post-widowhood experience, figuring out who you really want to spend time becoming more deeply involved with is what dating is all about. There is a smorgasbord of men out there. Both online and in real life. You date them, you narrow down the options, you figure out who is the best kisser, who sets your heart aflutter, who gets your panties in a bunch, who understands your mind, body, and soul, and who you could take home for Thanksgiving dinner.

I really don't want to know if my date from last Friday is saying cute things to the girl who works at the counter at the gourmet pizza place. We are adult human beings. We are not enslaved. We are allowed to flirt. And if he's a lying, cheating idiot, he will show his true colors. And I won't have a single doubt that it's time to say good-bye.

I just don't need to have some Internet dating site rubbing it in my face, when I really have no claims to the person. Yet. And I don't want the two or three men I'm casually dating to know I answered an email from some cute windsurfing instructor at one a.m. Please. Have we, as single people paying actual money to be part of an online dating site, no rights to our privacy?

I prefer real-life dating. Where what goes on at the deli counter, stays at the deli counter. Sometimes when you're dating, ignorance can be bliss.

BRA UNHOOKING 101

Six degrees of coordination

It's a Tuesday night. I am out on a date. I am out on a boat dock. In the moonlight. With boats bobbing all around me. And I am with one of my favorite kissing partners of all time, Professor W. And we are kissing and kissing and kissing, and he reaches under my chocolate brown cashmere sweater, and under my finely woven white cotton blouse and, suddenly—pop! My bra is unhooked. This has taken approximately one-fifth of a second. A blink of the eye. No fuss, no muss. Snap. Flip. Poof. It's unlatched.

It's a Wednesday afternoon. I am in a loft in town. Not to sound like a woman with no morals or conscience…but I am kissing someone else. It is thirteen hours later. I am wearing the same bra. I know, how could I? Well, I could. It's not as if I didn't shower or change my other clothing from the night before. I do have good hygiene. Last night was just a date with a little innocent kissing out on a boat dock. No nudity involved. This is different. This is a man I keep breaking up with and getting back together with. And we have a much deeper relationship than Professor W and I. I am not sleeping with both of them, for goodness sake. Stop making that face.

So, it is thirteen hours later, and it is the same bra, and I am trying to recall having soldered the hooks together in the interim hours, because this man cannot for the life of him get it undone. There is a struggle going on. He is engaged in battle with my bra closure. There is a moment when the romance just falls to the wayside and it is suddenly an all-out war. Man vs. bra. And the pale blue, lacy bra is clearly winning.

Finally, it comes to that point of utter defeat. That moment when the woman has to just reach back there and do the dirty work. Take charge of the situation. For God's sake! How can something so innocuous as a bra hook cause so much distress and pose such a challenge to an otherwise overly competent man? In my head, I am saying, *How can this be so difficult for you? Professor W got this unhooked in a fifth of a second just thirteen hours ago.* I am also thinking, *You really need some lessons from Professor W.*

Maybe it's because the professor does fine woodworking in his spare time. Or has unhooked the bras of hundreds of other women before me. But really, it doesn't matter. Because I think Professor W's manual dexterity is totally hot. And there is something way cool about having your bra unhooked on a public boat dock without anyone else being the wiser. Had the other man attempted to do the same, I am certain I would have ended up in the water, still wearing a closely fastened, lacy, light blue bra.

And there would have been a frustrated and embarrassed man, throwing me a life preserver.

DR. TALL, DARK, AND NAUGHTY

Finding Internet bliss in two short weeks

Try this: say *bad-boy doctor*. If you're a certain type of woman, it can be an intoxicating combination of words. Clearly, I am that type of woman, because as soon as I learned that, in addition to being a doctor, my date also had a slightly sordid past, well that was it for me. I was hooked.

I'd signed up for Match.com and, within two short weeks, found what I thought to be the answer to my dreams: Dr. Tall, Dark, Handsome—and apparently, based on his admission to having once been "laid off" temporarily from his medical duties due to a little run-in with the police involving possession of illegal, mind-altering substances—Naughty. I thought, *Wow, look at that! Only two weeks and I have found Mister (Could Be) Right. That was certainly worth the membership fee!*

Our entire relationship consisted of a goodly number of emails, a lot of telephone time, and a few dates. Our first date took place after only a couple of short conversations. I happened to be away in Newport with a close girlfriend. It was a lovely October weekend and we were celebrating my birthday in the year following Drew's death. It was a difficult one, and I'd arranged this weekend with my friend to keep me from feeling alone and sorry for myself.

My suitor and I arranged to meet in a quaint little town not too far from Newport. We had plans to go antiquing, look at art, and enjoy a bite of lunch. So Sunday afternoon my girlfriend took off for home and I took off for my first real date in approximately two decades.

At one point, I was pretty certain I was going to throw up and nearly had to pull the car over to the side of the road. Fortunately, I didn't. Instead, I overcame my nausea as I neared my destination using a little trick a Match.com-savvy friend had taught me: Call your date as soon as you are within two miles of your meeting destination and stay on the phone with him until you make eye contact.

Hopefully, you won't end up running into or over him.

It worked wonders. I just talked with him on my cell phone until he saw my car and I saw *him*. The ice is broken, and you are not left to wander up and down the sidewalk, wondering which pedestrian is your date. I still use the cell phone method of making an easy dating entrance. It helps you segue nicely from the car ride to the actual meeting of the date. Plus, if you see him and he looks like an ax murderer, well, you can always just keep driving and pretend you lost your cell reception.

Anyway, back to my first date story.

We had a lovely first date. I recall wandering around this quaint little town and going in and out of shops with him—charming shops filled with antiques and art. I kept glancing over at him and thinking, *I could kiss him*. As we strolled through town, it was just all too easy and comfortable. I felt as if we were performing in some well-choreographed dance. A ballet. It was enchanting. Every time I'd turn or spin, he'd be in just the right place—his hand touching my elbow, or softly alighting upon my shoulder or the back of my neck. It was a perfect first foray into the world of Internet dating.

Date number two was just as good. Well, almost. Were it not for the seven-mile hike through the woods during which we nearly had to call the state park patrol to rescue us, it would have been perfect. OK, in truth, the hike was a bit long, and his big, drooly dog came along with us, but still, we stopped and kissed a lot. Did I mention that he was a great kisser? Even now, when I scroll through the kissing pool in my mind, he probably ranks up there in the top ten.

I was lucky, because had he been an awful kisser, I might have stopped dating immediately and not started up again for quite a good, long time.

I had decided early on that the bad-boy doctor had all the right credentials to be not only my first real kissing partner A.D. (after Drew), but my first real sex partner, as well. He was such a great kisser, I thought it best to just get the whole thing over with so I could say I had done it, and move on. I was afraid that if I put it off for much longer, I would *never* be able to get naked with another man again in my lifetime. So, I just jumped in and did it.

It was a last-minute plan. I drove to his beautifully renovated house. He was childless for the weekend, and I was child-free for about thirty-six hours. (My children were staying with relatives overnight.) Managing to be free of my three cherubs so that I could go off for an overnight was no small feat, but I was determined to have sex. And when I set my mind to something, I make it happen. For better or worse.

The ensuing litany of disaster went something like this:

7:00 p.m.—I arrived and got a tour of the house.

7:59—We cooked and ate a delicious dinner together.

9:18—I noticed that he couldn't concentrate on kissing me until the dinner dishes were are all done. (This should have been red flag number one.)

9:44—We finished the dishes.

10:00—Some really good kissing in front of a romantic, roaring fire.

10:35—*He has asthma??! Who knew? Get the inhaler!*

11:00—I'd spent 20 minutes at home picking out the perfect lingerie, but he ripped it off of my body without even taking a look at it. (This should have been red flag number one-and-a-half.)

11:55—It's a long, cold, painfully self-conscious ascent up the antique staircase to the third-story bedroom when a man who has never seen you naked up until now is two feet behind you. It's even more painful if you are two feet behind *him*. This is more visual information than you need to possess this early in the game.

Midnight—I climbed into his comfy bed, only to have

the pillows ripped from under my head moments later while he muttered something about these being pillow *shams* and just decorative. (Obviously this should have been red flag number two.)

12:20 a.m.—Is it acceptable to pee while your date is brushing her teeth in your bathroom for the first time? I think not. I was married for fourteen years and one of the reasons we still were hot for one another was in no small part because we understood the importance of keeping certain things, like bodily functions, private. I'd known this man for approximately two weeks, had had three dates, and yet he thought nothing of peeing while I brushed my teeth. *Brushed my teeth*, for God's sake! Yuck. I remember spitting into the sink, looking up into the mirror and seeing him not three feet behind me. Peeing. (Red flag number three.)

1:00—I made love with the first new man in a long, long time.

I will skip this, for the most part. (Hint: It was disappointing, unimaginative and very, very…brief. And he certainly wouldn't have garnered the *I Try My Best* award.)

3:00—I made love for the second time with the first new man in a long time. (See above.)

3:09–7:00—I pretended to sleep while yearning to get up and go home.

7:00—"Who's my pretty girl?"

When you wake up in a new man's bed, especially for

the first time, you do not want to hear this question. Part of you is praying that he is, indeed, making lovey-dovey talk to his dog who, for some reason, needs to sleep in the same room. Even though the house is large enough for the dog to have its own bedroom. On its own floor. You do not want to believe that this man is saying something so saccharine and syrupy to you—so condescending and juvenile. But, another part of you is lying there, thinking, *Is he saying that to his dog? Am I not just as pretty as his smelly dog??*

7:42—*Could you please wait until I'm at least out of the bed before you start washing the sheets?* I got up to use the bathroom and returned to find he already had the bed mostly stripped and I could hear the washing machine revving up down the hall. (I guess the wash-the-dishes-before-we-can-have-sex mandate should have clued me in to his cleanliness obsession.)

8:12—I got dressed to make a quick escape while counting the minutes to my departure and planning my revenge. (I had stayed up half the night having sex with a man who didn't seem to even wonder, at any point, whether or not I was enjoying myself. At all. I was not used to such blatant selfishness and I wasn't going to sit back and take it.)

Lance Romance offered a trunk load of well-seasoned firewood when I left—in lieu of the unproffered cup of coffee that would have been the usual bare minimum of politeness before my long drive home. I sweetly and coyly went along with his smoochy-poochy love talk and little nuzzles, while all along I was seething—completely (and I do mean *completely*) unfulfilled and sleep-deprived. A half-cord of firewood was the least he could do.

I climbed into my SUV, put the window down, and kissed him good-bye. And I smiled sweetly as I pulled away…the smell of seasoned hardwood filling my vehicle.

Upon my arrival home, I first made a fire and then wrote him an email very nicely enlightening him that women actually enjoy orgasms too, and that I had not been there in bed with him the previous evening just to stay warm.

Surprisingly, he and his enormous ego (and believe me, that was the only thing that was oversized) did not take my comments and suggestions all that well.

Sadly, I no longer have a record of his precise reply, due to a few child-generated computer crashes and data losses over the years, but I believe his initial response was the classic no response at all. I then began to wonder whether I'd been a bit too harsh, and sent a follow-up email with a more heartfelt description of the reasons for my sexual disappointment. Which, interestingly, only caused his ego to be further wounded.

Apparently, women who date surgeons rarely, if ever, have the balls to tell them when they are awful in bed. My subsequent research dating men in the medical field has continued to support this theory.

I still sometimes wax nostalgic over his kissing, and the way he touched my elbow when we were out on that first date. I do not, however, find myself missing anything else.

THE ETIQUETTE BOYS

Nice boys order last

I like men with good manners. I don't care if it sounds old-fashioned to a lot of twenty-first-century women. I think good manners are part of the package. Drew had good manners. I have found that men who truly respect women usually also hold doors open for them and help them on with their coat. I like it when a man helps me on with my coat. And opens doors for me. And performs those little chivalrous acts happily.

I never realized the importance of good manners in a man until I was left husbandless and was forced to reenter the wild world of dating. Surprisingly, good manners have absolutely nothing to do with a man's age. I have dated younger men—men whose ages I will not even admit for fear their mothers might find and reprimand me—who had surprisingly good manners. And I have dated men my own age or older who showed a definite lack of chivalry. I have dated a man twenty years younger than myself who held the door open for me when we went to a burger place, and I have dated a man ten years older than myself who picked food out of his teeth as we sat in an upscale restaurant, drinking a $160 bottle of wine.

I dated one particular man who, although only a few years my junior, didn't seem to have gotten the hang of it. He rarely held doors open for me, and he certainly didn't help me on with my coat. On one occasion, at a museum in New York, I had to fetch my own coat while he waited in the lobby.

I had been trying to convince myself that his lack of gentleman-liness really didn't bother me. But as I stood there on that cold evening, having just tipped the coat check girl with the last dollar or two in my wallet, I had a small epiphany. As I twirled around, my right arm flailing in the air as I tried to get it inside the sleeve of my heavy wool coat without becoming entangled in my lengthy scarf while also keeping my purse from falling to the floor, I noticed them: the couple behind me. There he was, gently holding her coat and slipping it around her shoulders as her arms slid effortlessly into the sleeves. Unlike me, she looked…graceful. And he looked like a properly attentive date who wanted to help her look graceful.

It reminded me of the way Drew used to be there for me, in subtle, gentlemanly, quiet ways. And I glanced out into the lobby at my date, and my eyes got a bit watery, because this guy just didn't get it. He didn't have those instinctive good manners. And in that moment, I missed Drew for an entirely new reason. And I felt another kind of subtle emptiness. Once again, realizing that I had taken too much for granted.

The manners thing was most definitely a factor in the breakup equation.

Shortly after this, I got a report from Holden's first-grade teacher. During a class discussion of the importance of good manners on the playground, and about treating people and friends nicely, apparently my son felt the need to inject a bit of his mother's hard earned dating wisdom. He raised his hand and the teacher called on him, not suspecting what she was about to unleash. Holden then proceeded to enlighten the entire class with the news that manners were *very* important. That the man his mother had been dating did *not* have good manners. And that I had gotten rid of him, as a direct result of these bad manners. According to his teacher, he had told his seven-year-old classmates in no uncertain terms, "It is very important to have good manners. Trevor didn't, so now he can't be part of our family!"

Ouch.

By the way, my son has always let me order before him when we go out for chicken fingers and french fries. And the other day, I saw him hold open the door at the grocery store for an elderly woman.

It must be genetic.

LOVE, MARRIAGE...

Horse, carriage—whatever

After being involved in a variety of dating situations with a variety of men, and after experiencing a variety of levels of frustration, I eventually realized something that was rather disturbing. And very sad.

Many men have been married, many men have ended up divorced, yet many of these men have never really been in love. They got married, but they weren't head-over-heels, madly and passionately in love. Never. Not even on their wedding day. This was shocking to me. Truly. I suppose I just always imagined that all people felt the way that Drew and I felt about one another when we tied the proverbial knot.

The first time I realized this was when I had a man telling me he loved me, and yet he still thought it was OK to date other women. He honestly loved me, and he honestly believed that it was possible to love different people, for different reasons. He believed that we were all too possessive in our culture. That you could sleep with one person and profess your love on a Tuesday evening, then sleep with an entirely different person and profess your love on a Friday evening. Without it diminishing your love for the Tuesday person.

Now, my theory was a bit different. First of all, I told him that perhaps he needed to move to a location where this concept was more widely accepted and prevalent. Like the Middle East or Salt Lake City. Secondly, I believed that if you really loved the Tuesday person, you wouldn't want to sleep with the Friday person.

More importantly, I believed that if you truly loved the Tuesday person, you wouldn't want to imagine him or her making love with their very own Friday person. A bit of jealousy is not a bad thing. If someone is professing their love for me, I expect them to be a bit distressed at the thought of my having sex with another man. That is normal.

That is what makes you feel wanted and loved.

There were certain men who made me begin to doubt myself. Men who made me wonder whether maybe I was the one who was behind the times, out of the loop, a veritable dating "relic." Out of the singles world for such a lengthy period of time that I was still hanging on to antiquated ideas and impossibly high expectations. I mean, was it wrong and ridiculous to expect a man who professed to like me very much, or adore me, or even love me, to want *only* me?

Was "hooking up" the name of the dating game now, with no

possibility of true love? Didn't men and women still hold hands and stare into one another's eyes across a dinner table, and melt when they kissed goodnight? Didn't anyone just want to be with one person? For as long as it lasted—whether it turned out to be one week, one month, one year, or one lifetime? Had the word *smitten* been erased from the dictionary?

I truly began to wonder whether I was expecting the impossible.

But no, I am not expecting the impossible. Because I have been in love. I know what that feels like. You want one person, and the rest fall by the wayside. You want to kiss that person, and make love with that person, and snuggle with that person, and do silly, everyday little things with that person. You want to talk on the phone with that person late at night, so their voice is the last thing you hear before you drift off to dreamland.

You don't want sex with someone else, because you are in love.

GOOD VIBRATIONS

One of the bad things about losing Drew (besides the obvious) was that we had always been a great match, sexually. And suddenly, he was gone. And with him went the great sex.

Even worse, however, was that after he was gone and I began dating (and being naked with) other men, I realized our sex life could have, indeed, probably been even better.

Married on the cusp of my twenty-seventh birthday, and with Drew only a year-and-a-half ahead of me, we spent our shared thirties navigating a decade's worth of pregnancies, diaper changing, and toddler chasing. Finally, when I was thirty-eight, with our youngest son on the other side of his first birthday, and the Holy Grail on the horizon—a return of our physical energy and possibly even a back-to-normal sex drive—the whole terminal cancer thing came knocking and put more than a slight damper on things.

Just when most couples would have been celebrating a return to the sex life of their courtship days, or possibly even a more fulfilling one, we were slammed into cancer hell.

And to be honest, terminal cancer is just not sexy.

It might make you both feel emotionally closer, it may make you want to be physically closer and make love more often, knowing the time you have may be limited. But it's no longer sex of the "reckless abandon" variety. The sheer joy is sucked out of it, much the same way it is sucked out of many of life's other previously simple and taken-for-granted pleasures. It's sex with a new level of depth, but also sex that is covered with a veil of unspoken sadness. Or, at the very least, melancholy.

It used to make me want to cry, at times. I'd try to remain in the moment, to enjoy the sex. The closeness. The orgasms. But it was never the same as before. At that juncture, I was just thrilled to have one more night in my beloved's arms. The last thing I was thinking about was spicing up our sex life with something out of a sex toy catalogue.

When I was married, I owned one vibrator. And I don't even recall where it came from. For all I know, it could have come with the cherished 1870s house we had purchased during my second pregnancy, like the vintage pottery bowls we found in our ancient basement, or the weathered, wooden Coca-Cola ruler we found behind that shelf in the kitchen. The ruler that now sits in my kitchen here in Maine and gently reminds me to "Do unto others as you would have them do unto you." (A sentiment that many men would do well to remember before climbing into bed with me.)

I don't recall ever needing a vibrator when I was married. Or really wanting to use one—even for fun, playful, married-sex purposes. Either I was too inhibited at the time to even think of using it as a twosome or, a more likely scenario, I was too tired to mess with something that was already working just fine without the aid of battery-powered devices.

But since my widowhood, I confess, my vibrator collection has increased significantly. For better or for worse, I've discovered that many men are much more open about sex and toys than I ever anticipated. I'm not a sex toy aficionado; I tend to like the simpler pleasures. Maybe it's just that I'm an artist and a writer—whatever happened to using your imagination? What happened to improvisation? For me, having a closet full of vibrators is like being a little girl with seventeen different versions of Barbie. When did people stop buying the basic Barbie and dressing her in different outfits?

A man once gave me an impressive, intelligent, yet sexy-looking little vibrator on a first date. I recall plunking down into a comfy chair out in a public locale and, before I could even take a sip of my wine, he handed me a small, decorative shopping bag. Inside I found a small box which looked like it might hold a fancy bar of soap. Or a bottle of perfume. But no. Opened, the box contained a marvel of Swedish sex toy technology. Were it up to the single women of the world, I think it would have won the Nobel

Peace Prize.

Who would have expected a vibrator on a first date? Not me. I think Drew gave me a small stuffed animal on our fourth date. This was an entirely new ball game.

At first, I wasn't sure whether being gifted with a sexual aid (before even having sex) was a subtle message that a man was (a) bad in bed, (b) lazy, or (c) merely very interested in my sexual pleasure.

After many more years of research, I've found that the meaning seems to depend upon the man and his choice of sexual aid. Clearly, a gentleman who gives you something to pleasure yourself with offers more hope than some dude who gives you a nurse's outfit (with a stethoscope) and some electronic device that is quite obviously purchased for the central purpose of *his* pleasure.

Please. Go back to your man cave.

So suddenly, barely a handful of years after Drew's untimely death, I found myself doing things with men on third dates that I hadn't done with my own husband in my entire twenty-two years of knowing him.

My expanding experience of "sex after Drew" was enlightening but also made my heart ache a bit more. The bulk of my body and soul has always just wished that he could return from the great beyond. Rise from the dead. At times, I've wished I would wake up in my bed in the middle of the night and find him there, just so I could tell him about all of the wonderfully liberating and fun things we had in our younger days perhaps been a bit too shy to try. Or about subjects and desires we had been too timid to broach with one another.

It's not just vibrators and other pleasure-enhancing devices that have made sex more fun. I still truly treasure the basics of great sex, without any help from a man-made object—vibrating or not. The new element is the fearlessness, the confidence, the willingness and curiosity that just wasn't there when I was younger. Once you have that, you can do with it what you want. Use it for good, or a bit of devilishly fun evil. Or not at all.

What's that Star Trek motto: "To boldly go where no man has gone before"?

Well for me, and for a few of the men I've been with, that has turned out to be quite literal.

It's not that I'm sad thinking back on our sex life, or that I feel as if it could have been all that much improved. It's just that, as with my discovery of my love of writing, or my moving to a vintage house on the ocean, I wish he were here to share in my new revelations and discoveries. My new awakenings. My new life.

Because, man oh man, we'd sure be having some fun.

PENISES

They come in all shapes and sizes

The feeling I had when I met Drew on our first day of college remains forever burned into my memory. I took one look at him, saw one smile, heard one sentence come from his mouth, and I was hopelessly smitten. We didn't date seriously until two years later, each of us having had others to whom we were still romantically attached. But believe me, I knew he was the one I wanted to end up with one day.

Although we had kissed and done some of the proverbial collegiate "fooling around" while we were freshmen, we didn't have sex until our junior year, after we had confessed, and professed, our love to one another. (Mom, I hope you're not reading this!) On that night, we made love for the first time. And I had an orgasm in about seven seconds. Considering the fact that, prior to this experience, I'd been having sex with my first boyfriend for approximately seven months before I even knew one could achieve an orgasm via intercourse alone, this was an enlightening development, to say the least. And of course, I was already in love with Drew, so this was just an added (and very lovely) bonus.

Although I hadn't had an abundance of sexual experience prior to Drew, it didn't take much to imagine that he probably fell outside of the "average" realm—not just in terms of endowment but in terms of heart, soul, character, and in any other ways that counted. He not only had been blessed but he knew what to do with his blessings. And no, I'm not just saying that because he's dead and I've put him upon a pedestal. I have, reluctantly, had opportunity to conduct this post-widowhood survey and have determined that he really was quite special.

After he died, and after I found the strength, desire and, let's face it, the courage to begin dating, I was in for a shock. Beyond the bizarre reality that I had to get naked with new men after having been with the same one for so many years was an even more disconcerting realization: I had to be with an entirely new batch of penises, as well.

The entire nudity thing was troubling enough. Not just the man's, but my own. Getting naked with someone when you're in your forties is not the same as getting naked with someone when you're nineteen. Or even thirty-one. Especially someone who had not fathered your children. Or watched as you gave birth to his nine pound, eleven ounce prodigy. As I once read somewhere, if you find a middle-aged woman crying after the man she's been dating has just broken up with her, it's probably not because she's heartbroken. More likely it's because she now faces the prospect of having to get naked in front of yet one more new man.

But, getting back to penises, when you haven't been with a new one in quite some time, you tend to forget that they're not all created equal.

They come in all shapes and sizes. Short. Long. Fat. Skinny. Crooked. Straight. Some men know what to do with them—and some, clearly, do not.

When you mostly date men over the age of forty, the attached penises also, more and more often, come in a variety of, shall we say, degrees of firmness. Much like tofu: Soft. Firm. Extra-firm. Some are tricky: they're firm for a few seconds and then— *whoops*—not so much anymore. I had not been used to being with a man who experienced technical difficulties. Ever. Well, unless he'd had a bit too much to drink and fell asleep before his claims to want to make love were realized. But even then, I'm pretty certain he could have still managed to have sex, even while half asleep, had I asked him politely.

Although I've not had much personal experience with men in

my age range enlisting the aid of Viagra, I have been with one or two who definitely could have benefited from the use of some type of pharmaceutical cheerleading. Because when sex lasts for less time than it takes to open the condom packaging, there is a problem. I've also been with one man who, in retrospect, was probably "using." Had I been nosey enough to peek into his medicine cabinet while I was brushing my teeth on any given evening, I'd have undoubtedly found the hard evidence. Because when sex lasts for more time than it takes to watch *Titanic*, there is an entirely different type of problem. More is not always better.

Penises all seem to have their own little quirks, too. Their own personalities. Rarely do you find one that they might use as a model, for say, a sex toy. I think I was married to one like that, and didn't fully realize it. Much like Goldilocks I'd found one that was "just right." And along with other things that I took for granted—things like his smile and his ability to make me laugh, even when I was in the most foul of moods—I had taken his penis for granted. Damn.

After a number of intimate experiences over the years with men I was dating, this new revelation was a real downer. I know it will sound difficult to believe, but prior to my first experience with a new one, I really hadn't given the penis thing too much thought. The kissing and underwear issues had occupied my widowed brain and possessed my thoughts for so long that what lay beyond that seemed almost superfluous.

Thank goodness I didn't give it too much thought, or I'd have really needed antidepressants.

OK, Drew, you can stop laughing now.

INTERNET DATING DÉJÀ VU

Two halves don't make a whole

Journal entry

12 November 2007

10:19 p.m.

It is now approximately two months and three weeks since my reentry into the hell of Internet dating. And, make no mistake about it...it is hell.

So, let's see...what progress have I made in my love life? What great leaps have I taken? After only five short days on the Internet, I found (or, shall I say, was found by) two perfect men. Well, seemingly perfect men. The first was a sex god who could make me come constantly... but couldn't make me laugh. The second made me laugh constantly, but couldn't make me come. He barely even tried. If only I could have performed a mind-meld between the two of them, I would have had Mr. Absolutely-Hilariously-Fucking-Perfect. I would have become an official Match.com spokesperson and gone to bed every night with a smile on my face and a giggle on my lips.

Sadly, no one has yet figured out how to perform a mind-meld between two men who possess the important qualities you are searching for. In two separate bodies.

Sex or witty banter? Witty banter or sex? Why must a

woman choose? I want both. At once. I do not want witty banter on Friday night and hot sex on Saturday night. I want both. On Sunday morning. Dammit.

Back to hanging out at the BMW dealership, waiting for some man who smells really good and owns silver cufflinks to walk in for an oil change.

I really do hate dating.

MY GREAT ASS

It's all in the genes…or the jeans

I never thought of myself as having a great behind. I mean, I always knew I had a nice body. But I also recall having layered eight pair of cotton underwear under my jeans (at age thirteen) before going to dinner at some friend of the family's house because they had a cute son my age and I wanted my derriere to appear more, well, prevalent.

Let's just say that I never thought of my ass as my greatest asset.

So imagine my surprise when I began dating again after Drew died only to have men making proclamations left and right about what a "great ass" I had.

I knew Drew liked my behind. But I am not even certain that *he* ever told me I had a great ass. Maybe he did, maybe I just didn't really give it much credence since he was my husband and he was supposed to think I was wonderfully perfect in all ways.

So here I was, with men drooling all over me and my great behind. At first, I didn't really believe it. But when I started hearing it not only from dates 1, 2, and 3…but also from dates 4, 5, 6, 7, 8, 9, 10, and 11, I began to think, *Huh. Maybe I really* do *have a great ass!* I mean, what could make a forty-something woman happier than to find out the ass she thought was just passable for her first four decades was now something to be coveted—something men were dreaming about when they climbed into bed at night?

I soon came to the conclusion that my ass wasn't all that spectacular. It was the jeans. Or the way my ass fit into the particular jeans I had inadvertently purchased. When I came to this realization, I began wearing the same pair of jeans on each and every first date, just to test my theory. I had a kind of first date uniform, to keep the testing ground consistent. I mean, I wanted to be comparing apples to apples, so to speak. So, the "great ass jeans," a thin cashmere sweater, silver earrings, and upswept hair. That was my first date uniform. Upswept hair because I suddenly also had every man telling me what a beautiful neck I had. (I had previously always disliked my neck. Now I was appreciating both my ass and my neck more and more every day.)

Then I did what any woman would have done. I went out and bought five more pair of the exact same jeans, just in case they were discontinued at any point down the road. I wore those jeans constantly. I wore them until they all were full of tears and holes and until the belt loops were all in varying degrees of disintegration from being twisted around men's fingers while they pushed me up against car doors and restaurant walls and kissed me goodnight. Those were some jeans. Now I only have one pair left, and they are too ragged to wear out of the house. I am going to keep them and frame them and display them on my bedroom wall when I get too old to remember how to have sex.

In the meantime, I have come to the conclusion that, although I exercise and use the elliptical torture machine faithfully and walk and do all of that good butt-shaping stuff, I still do not have a truly great ass. I think that what I am blessed with is precisely the right amount of material in that area, and when it is squeezed into the right pair of pants, well it gives the illusion of being nearly perfect. The problem is, eventually, you have to get naked.

R-E-S-P-E-C-T

At one point, after being on my tour-of-dating for a while, I had had sex just three times in the past year. With the same person. Once every four months, approximately. And it wasn't even that good. This so saddened me, that I was moved to write a New Year's Eve appeal and email it to all my female friends and relatives. An appeal to help me find a man. So that on the eve of the next new year I would have a much higher number to report.

All I had been thinking about for nearly a full year was sex. And that I would really like to be having it three times a day, not three times a year. And how difficult it was to find a man I would even want to imagine being naked with.

Naturally, it stands to reason that the next man I would find myself attracted to and involved with would be a man who refused to have sex with me. How could this be? He claimed to be attracted to me. He called me constantly—and I mean every *day*, at least once. We had fun together. We laughed together. He told me how hot I was. He eventually kissed me (and, although not great at first, with a bit of intervention, it turned into relatively decent kissing). So we had gotten to the kissing. But he would not have sex with me. He would not do anything with me. He wanted me to respect his desire to put off being physically intimate.

Now, I like being old-fashioned. I like being smart. I think putting off sex is not a bad way to proceed. But, it took him three months to kiss me. This led me to believe that, if I went along with his plan…it was entirely possible that we might not be having sex until the spring of 2017. And who knew if it would be worth the wait?

I thought a preview of some sort was not an unreasonable expectation.

Nonetheless, he wanted to "wait." For what, I am not sure. Perhaps for some sign from God. Like in that movie, where the divorced American woman wants to buy the villa in Tuscany… but the little old superstitious Italian lady who owns it is waiting for a sign, to know that it is the right buyer for the house. And then a bird poops on the divorced American woman's head and, Holy shit, there's the sign from God.

Draw up the purchase and sale agreement.

This man is part Italian, so maybe he was waiting for a bird to poop on my head or a miniature poodle to pee on my leg. I don't know. All I know is, he was the first man I had been attracted to, both mentally and physically, in a long, long time and he goes and pulls the "I think it's really important to just be really good friends first" routine. He talked and talked and talked. All talk. No action.

I once told him to "put out or shut up." He laughed. I didn't.

I wasn't kidding.

One day, I found an email in my in-box from some silly dating advice website. The subject heading was "What it means when he doesn't call." Well, duh. Any idiot knows what it means when he doesn't call. I thought about writing the site and asking what it means when he calls you constantly but won't have sex with you.

I am pretty sure the dating experts would have told me he was either:

- Gay and just doesn't know it yet, or

- Having major intimacy/commitment issues and requires extensive therapy

This was the same man who sent me mysterious text messages saying things like, "I'll call you when I…" *Wait! When you what?* He also tended to disappear on major holidays and then call to give his GPS coordinates and tell me he's hiding out from the world in some seedy little hotel while en route to who knows where.

He was also genetically incapable of making a plan for a date more than three-and-a-half hours in advance.

Since meeting me, he:

- Dropped his phone into a toilet, then lost it another two or three times

- Crashed his computer hard drive and nearly ended up in a mental facility

- Suffered three or four bouts of the flu, at least a dozen migraines, and a motorcycle accident

- Had an impending surgical procedure to his big toe constantly looming on the horizon like an enormous black cloud

Note that we are talking about toe surgery, not a heart transplant. As a woman whose late husband battled cancer and endured a six-hour surgical procedure in which half his digestive system was removed, it's difficult for me to feel much empathy for a man who hyperventilates over the thought of his big toe going under the knife.

My theory was that he liked me, but his fear of my pouncing upon him at some point and forcing him to participate in something resembling physical intimacy caused him to make these disasters manifest within his life—because they usually ended up interfering with our dates. It was clearly a subconscious defense mechanism at work, like a skunk's spray or a porcupine's quills.

I was the enemy. I wanted sex.

I once didn't hear from him for a few days, and wondered what had happened to his daily calls. I thought he was angry with me or something. Although I couldn't imagine why. Then I awoke one morning to find a string of lengthy text messages. From *him*.

It took me a while to realize that most of them weren't meant for me. And they didn't arrive in order. I cautiously began reading the first installment. It said something about missing me, and that he had always and would always care about me. I thought, *Oh. How sweet. He really does care about me.* Then, upon rumination, I thought it a bit of an odd sentiment, considering he had only known me three months. But, oh well, he had *always* cared about me. How sweet! I read the next text message with anticipation. I read slowly, letter by letter, as the words trickled down my tiny phone screen, and it said:

I want to see you, Torhilda. I miss the family in Oslo.

Torhilda? Who the hell is Torhilda? Oslo? I am not Torhilda. And I don't live in Oslo.

The next four text messages I had the pleasure to receive were in Norwegian. Apparently, I was the inadvertent recipient of his overseas text messages to his cousins. (I could not make this stuff up if I tried.) When I finally spoke with him later that day, I told him that I had received his messages meant for his relatives in Norway. I asked him if it was a joke. I told him I was going to use it in my screenplay someday. He told me that I could not under any circumstances use it in a screenplay. (I don't recall him saying I couldn't use it in a book, however. And he definitely never got me to sign any binding legal contract.)

Still, with no other dating prospects in sight, I continued to torment myself by staying in touch with him, while speculating and attempting to unravel both his odd behaviors and his true sexual leanings. If nothing else, he provided entertainment. For a while, of a sort.

Another man, another story.

THE LUCKY PHOTO

A picture is worth a thousand words,
and sometimes they're fiction

I once had a man tell me people thought he looked like Pierce Brosnan. The actor. The guy with the dark, wavy hair and the chiseled jaw. The guy who once played James Bond, 007. I liked him: the guy who told me he looked like Pierce Brosnan. He was a great writer. He was a great speller. In the photo he had posted he did not look unlike Pierce Brosnan. I decided to go out to dinner with him. In person, but for the dark wavy hair, he looked completely unlike Pierce Brosnan. C'est la vie.

Another man refused to send me a photo of himself. He emailed me and called me and wanted to meet me, but he would not send me a photo. Usually, I would not have continued talking with someone whose photo I had not seen. Much less agree to meet with him for lunch. But there was something about him. Something confident and a bit cocky. And, unfortunately, that always attracted me. Plus, I should mention that I put him through the wringer before meeting him, since he wouldn't send his photo. I got every detail of his appearance: inseam, waist size, shoe size, preference in ties, suit coat size, and whether or not he'd had braces in his youth. I knew it all. I could put together all of his measurements and vital statistics and I could come up with a visual.

The last thing he told me was that he looked "like Ben Affleck, but probably better looking." Now, I have never considered Ben Affleck to be my ideal. But he was dark and rather handsome, and he had been engaged to JLo, so how bad could he really be?

I googled Ben Affleck before agreeing to meet Mr. No Photo. I needed to remember what he really looked like. I googled. I looked. I drooled. I had not had a good kiss in quite a while. Ben Affleck was no slouch! And besides, I had a weakness for men with dark hair and dark eyes.

I signed up for the lunch date with Mr. No Photo.

Driving to the restaurant on the appointed weekday afternoon I was filled with anticipation. I conversed with him on my cell phone as I pulled around the back of the restaurant and into the parking lot. As he talked me in for my landing, I laughed nervously, because I didn't see him. I saw one man, standing on the sidewalk. On his cell phone. But I did not see Ben Affleck.

Of course it turned out the guy on the sidewalk was my lunch date.

I wanted to just keep going and drive right past him, straight out of the parking lot exit, back onto the highway. Back to my house, far from the Hollywood Hills. But I am too nice to do that. No. I parked. I feigned interest (well, a little interest). I mean, really, how much sympathy can you have for a man who compares himself to a movie star? And not just compares himself, but claims to be an even more handsome version of that same movie star. It's better to sell yourself a bit short and turn out to be a pleasant surprise rather than a disappointment.

If I've learned any life lesson on Match.com, it's this: Surprise and delight. Do not surprise and disappoint.

MRS. ROBINSON

I think I went to high school with your mother

When you are suddenly single, you suddenly have a world of dating possibilities at your feet. It's like being a college student all over again. Except for one thing: you generally have little in common with most college students. Or recent graduates.

When does a boy become a man? Or, rather, when does a boy start doing his own laundry? Obviously, not at age twenty-two.

I had met a lovely, and obviously much younger, gentleman on my Internet dating site of choice. He had sought me out, not vice versa, so I was not feeling icky or "cougarish" in the least. After exchanging a few emails, we made short work of meeting in person. Since he was the instigator, and I was merely the lucky recipient of his attentions, it was a no-brainer. The last time I had been with a twenty-two-year-old, the twenty-two-year-old was Drew. And we still had confetti stuck to our shoes from our college graduation. And so, I found myself dating a man who could have been my offspring—had I gotten pregnant at a more tender age.

Our first "date" was a meeting at my house. We sat in my living room and had long and meaningful talks about all manner of subjects. He was intelligent, articulate, surprisingly confident, and, not for nothing, really cute.

As he walked out the door to go home, we paused on my front porch in the rain and he kissed me. It was quite incredible. No doubt, the fact that we were on public display in my town filled with perfectly married, conformist people, and that our kissing was illuminated by my porch light, kicked everything up a few notches. I think he was shocked at how hot it was. That made two of us. My kids were asleep, and he and I proceeded to spend the next few hours in his car, creating enough steam to run a train from New York to Los Angeles.

Did I mention it was raining?

OK, so kissing someone I could have given birth to turned out to be not disturbing in the least. But the kissing and eventual nakedness wasn't the real cause of my ultimate distress.

When I thought of the delicious possibilities going out with a twenty-two-year-old held, I didn't think about the actual maturity level of said twenty-two-year-old. I thought only of his probably hairless chest, his taut body, and attractive sexual naïveté. I did *not* think about the fact that his mommy still probably made his breakfast before he jumped on the commuter train every weekday morning, and not only washed, dried, and folded his socks and underwear but most likely put them away in his drawer for him as well.

I got a bad feeling in the pit of my stomach the day after he went out shopping for a condo. He hadn't found anything in his price range, but it did provide a jumping-off point for me to learn more about him. Like the fact that his mother was planning to stop by and provide cleaning services once he procured his bachelor pad. I was shocked. Really? I mean, why would a mother want to turn herself into domestic help, and without pay? I mean, who are these women who still feel the need to play the mommy role to the no longer helpless baby boy, who is now having sex on a regular basis and quite able to not only shop for but use his very own can of Pledge? These women are obviously having a bit of their own separation anxiety, and a few identity crisis "issues." And as a woman who is now able to date their sons, I say to them, *grow up!*

So, to answer my own question, "When does a boy start doing his own laundry?" When his mommy allows him to become a man. Real men do their own laundry. Real women like men who do their own laundry. Mrs. Robinson would *never* have offered to do Benjamin's laundry.

In addition to the mommy issues, there was also the whole "religion" thing.

He was raised Catholic and was quite conservative, to boot. The difference in our religious beliefs and upbringings had given us much material for thoughtful discussion, and probably only added fuel to the sexual tension that already naturally existed between us. In my experience, there is no better foreplay than a hot debate over religion or politics.

So, although he was charming, his youthful Pope-induced guilt didn't become apparent until what shall always in my memory be known as The Purifying Gel Incident. After having sex with me for the first time, he disappeared into my bathroom for a good ten minutes or more and, from what I could later ascertain, had used half a bottle of my $26 dermatologist-dispensed facial cleanser, appropriately called Purifying Cleansing Gel.

To cleanse him of all of his sins, I am assuming. Oh. My.

I bet he had fun at Confession that Sunday.

After that, I realized that the novelty of the situation was already losing its charm. We'd pretty much explored as much of a relationship as was practical and it was probably best to keep my expensive facial cleanser for myself. Besides, I was going to be moving soon, and I certainly wasn't taking a twenty-two-year-old along with me…or folding his underwear.

GOOD-BYE GENERATION *OH, NO* — HELLO GENERATION O

I have been learning an inordinate number of interesting tidbits about men since I have been thrust (perhaps not the best word) back into this second round of dating, forty-something style. One of the most disconcerting and troubling things I have uncovered (again, maybe a better word is out there) is the number of men in my age category who are just not all that into the whole oral sex thing. Giving it. Getting it. Doesn't matter. They are just not into it. Or they never learned how. Or they are no longer flexible enough to get into the required positions to make it a positive experience for all concerned.

I once dated a man who consistently ruined the whole thing by making exclamations in the immediate aftermath of otherwise lovely oral sex experiences. Exclamations such as:

- "I think I have a concussion!"

- "I think I need a neck brace!"

- "Were you trying to suffocate me?!"

Or, my all-time favorite:

- "My eyes are stinging. Next time I think I need a scuba mask!"

Of course, this same man had apparently never heard of a woman who couldn't reach an orgasmic state of ecstasy after thirty seconds of intercourse alone. He clearly hadn't dated much or read any of the sex research reports. Had he checked out the existing data, he would have found that something like 80 percent of women cannot even *have* an orgasm via the act of intercourse on its own. Most of us need a combination of items from columns A, B, and C on the sexual menu to get that smile on our face.

Hello.

So, with that in mind, how do you think we're supposed to reach Nirvana? Not with your fingertips, dear, as agile as they may be. Think, think, think. Any other ideas pop into that cute little head of yours?

It especially irks me when a man loves to receive oral sex but is not enthusiastic about reciprocating. What is that all about? Didn't these men ever hear of the old adage "It is better to give than to receive?" I bet a woman coined that little gem. Haven't they heard of that fabulously fabulous book (written by a guy!) *She Comes First?*

I mean, these men are just not using their brains. Well, clearly. A woman who has been satisfied will not roll over and go to sleep like a man might. She will usually be so thrilled that a man has finally figured out the way it should work, she will be more than happy (*happy, happy!*) to show her appreciation.

In a million different ways. Creative ways. Delicious ways!

I have dated men in a wide age range, and it seems that younger men (especially much younger men) are a bit more enlightened about how the whole sex thing works. The whole oral sex thing, especially. Maybe it's because they were raised by a bunch of women who didn't put up with the ridiculousness in the bedroom that the mothers of the men who are my age most likely accepted as "normal" behavior. Good Lord. No wonder there are so many women my age who are so uptight and unhappy looking.

The younger women of today are going to be having a whole lot more fun, if this particular younger man I'm thinking of is any indication of the new generation of men. Generation O— for *orgasm*.

Scuba mask, indeed.

"OH MY GOD...I'VE BEEN NAKED HERE BEFORE"

When you date in a state as small as Maine (and a city as small as Portland) there is bound to be some potentially awkward dating overlap. I once experienced this overlap on a level that was both amusing and disturbing.

I was on my first date with a man who had been communicating with me for weeks, and we finally found a mutually agreeable time to get away from our respective children and meet in person. We'd probably already logged more hours of conversation than some married couples have in a lifetime, so I was feeling quite comfortable and trusting of him and his motives when we finally met. After a few hours together, chatting and laughing and kissing in my car, I suggested we go up to his place—

a condo in a charming and desirable part of the city. Had I not been so comfortable, I wouldn't have made this suggestion. But I was. So I did. It was really more about hanging out and being able to sit on his couch and be comfy than going up to his place to have sex or anything of that nature.

But the moment I followed him through his front door, sex was the only thing on my mind. Not sex with him. Sex with another man. A man who, I slowly realized, used to live in this very condo. That is the kind of déjà vu moment you just don't want to have on a first date with a potential love interest.

Pretending not to be having flashbacks of another man's naked body parts, I stood in the center of the room and soaked in the surroundings. Let's see, the bed used to be in the opposite corner, the bar and stereo system were in the spot now occupied by children's bunk beds. But, yes indeed. I was naked here before.

How could this be? What are the chances? It took a few days of covert investigation, but I ultimately discovered that the man I was now kissing owned said condo and had rented it to the man I had previously been kissing (and, obviously, more than that at one particular juncture) a year or so before, while in the midst of his divorce.

Could this happen in New York City? Or Boston? Or Chicago? Probably not.

Should I have gotten naked with man number 2 in the same condo where I'd been naked with man number 1? Probably not. Did I?

Of course.

PART THREE: New Self

10
FAITH AND SPIRITUALITY

GOD?

WHEN YOU FIND OUT your husband not only has cancer, but a cancer that is classified as terminal, you find God rather quickly.

You don't care where He or She is hiding or how long it's been since you've set foot in a church. You find God. You hunt Him down and you have a big long chat with Him. I myself swore at Him a lot, and begged, and bargained, and apologized.

I wasn't an atheist or anything like that before I heard the words *pancreatic cancer*, but I certainly also wasn't a veritable "church lady."

Suddenly, however, I was in constant contact with God. He was my new best friend. I'd pull over on my drive back home from dropping off our four-year-old at preschool, and I'd sob and talk to *Him* as I sat in my car on the side of the road. I'd be in the bathroom at Dana-Farber while Drew was having his insides irradiated, on line at the grocery store, on line at Starbucks. Changing diapers. Every place and every mindless activity provided an opportunity to have a little talk.

It was actually more pleading than talking. More of a one-sided conversation.

Then I realized that if God were really as sharp and all-knowing as He was reputed to be, He would see right through my new-found friendliness and know that my sudden change in attitude was due strictly to the fact that I wanted to save my husband. I mean, God can't be that stupid. He must get that stuff all the time from people who are hanging out at places like Dana-Farber.

In the end, I lost God. Or maybe I misplaced Him. It seemed like He'd been taken over by institutional religion, and that the only way to really get His attention was to play by the rules. So I looked toward ministers and church people for support. But I realized that in the end, we're pretty much in this alone. We looked to them for comfort, and sadly found out that the church "rules" were more important than the actual church members. Sure, it was fine when they were sending you quarterly statements to remind you of how much money you had pledged and what you still owed. It was fine when they were asking you to be a Sunday school teacher or to make cheesy ornaments out of felt and sequins for the holiday fair. But when you were in need, for the most part, they weren't much help.

CHECKING OUT OF THE GARDEN OF EDEN

When we found out about Drew's recurrence, it was August of 2002. He had been doing very well for nearly two-and-half years, and we truly believed that perhaps he had reached the "safe" zone. We thought he was, perhaps, one of the miracle survivors of pancreatic cancer. Of course, just as we began to allow that possibility to sink into our heads and hearts and souls, a routine MRI revealed our worst nightmare: the cancer had spread to his liver and lungs. It was difficult to even absorb this news, much less say the words aloud to anyone else, thereby making it all too real.

When we called our beloved minister, who had been very close to us and a great source of strength for Drew, we found out the hard way that religious red tape sometimes overrides simple human kindness.

During the course of Drew's illness, a lot of moving had gone on. We had relocated to a new town, and our minister had also moved on—to a new church. These two events propelled us into a time of churchlessness. We didn't want to make the thirty-five-minute trek back to our old church, and the fact that our minister was no longer there removed any last shred of incentive we might have had to drag our children and ourselves out of our cozy beds early on a Sunday morning.

Apparently, church rules dictated that because he had switched parishes, we weren't "allowed" to talk with him, he was not allowed to return our calls, and we were told (by his dogma-loving wife) that Drew needed to contact the temporary "replacement" minister at our old church. A person we had never laid eyes on.

Basically, we were screwed. I tried to imagine God having sat down over coffee one morning and come up with this kind of ridiculousness, and it was a rather difficult scenario to envision.

> *Doris, please get out your steno pad. Article 5, section B, paragraph 16 should read as follows: "All communication with the terminally ill must be suspended should the dying person and/or minister switch towns and/or churches." And be sure to run that by our attorney first. We don't want any lawsuits.*

So there we were, in the depths of despair, cut off from our religious security blanket. I could barely pass this news along to Drew, for fear of sending him over the edge of the cliff from which he was already dangling. Meanwhile, I was on a seesaw, vacillating between sobs of sadness and fits of swearing at Mr. Sinister Minister and his witch of a wife. In between my tears, all that kept going through my head was, *Is this what Jesus would have recommended? What the hell is wrong with these fucking people?*

About three months later, when Drew was nearly in death's waiting room, we at last received a letter from our former minister, trying to make amends. I always wondered whether he was mostly attempting to relieve his own guilt before Drew actually passed away and was no longer around to accept his olive branch.

My instinct was to ignore the olive branch. Or burn it.

But of course the only thing that mattered was Drew, and that the note comforted him and offered him a bit of peace. I myself was not really in the mood to make all nicey-nice, although I put on a good act. I was determined to be supportive. Even if I had to bite my own tongue.

Of course, after Drew's death, the fact that the very same minister who had abandoned him in his hours of greatest need—all in the name of church-related bureaucracy, rules, and red tape—officiated at his funeral was surreal to me. But he was the most familiar thing we had to cling to at the time, minister-wise, and I knew that Drew had forgiven him so I went along with it, too. In reality, it took many more years for my heart to truly soften and reach a state of forgiveness.

Of course, I didn't really think much about the entire minister issue in the aftermath of Drew's death. Extraordinary grief pretty much supersedes any other of life's little irritations.

In the end, the whole experience truly taught me that we are all just people. And special costumes and titles and a fancy diploma from a divinity college doesn't make you any better than any other human being.

It taught me to always follow my heart. Not the rules.

Because I'm pretty sure Jesus would have returned Drew's call.

I've learned some painful lessons, but it has helped me to grow as a human being. I no longer rely on an organized religion to bolster, sustain, or approve of me. I no longer think that anyone needs to act as a middleman between me and my God. I discovered that I didn't need to go looking for God. God was within Drew, myself, and our three beautiful children. He was in us and with us all the time.

I no longer fear death, because I saw the man I love face it with grace and dignity. The same way he faced life. I watched him take his last breath and smile his last smile. I felt his last kiss. I saw his body, lying there like an empty shell. And I realized one wonderful thing. He clearly wasn't his body. He wasn't there. He was somewhere else. Death is a doorway, and no amount of time sitting in any church could have ever truly taught me that. Drew taught me that. Having the privilege of being beside him, being a witness to the end of his life, taught me that.

And it is a gift and a lesson that has changed my life...forever.

THE VANISHING NATIVITY

Misplacing Jesus

I kept living in the house that we had shared with Drew for quite a while after he died. After two years, however, I knew I had to get the hell out of there. Unless I wanted to torment myself forever. Maybe if he hadn't died there, it would have been more bearable. But he had in fact died there, and it definitely was not bearable.

When we packed up our house in preparation for our move to Maine, I decided to sort through our holiday stuff (which, at the time, was mostly in cardboard boxes that were about to disintegrate) and move it all into those handy-dandy new and improved storage containers. Those big clear plastic bins with the jelly bean-colored lids. You know, Tupperware on steroids.

I thought I could accomplish three tasks at once: sorting, purging, and reorganizing.

It was a difficult trio of tasks, to say the least. Every Christmas ornament was a reminder of Drew's demise and that last holiday season together.

Every piece of tinsel was like a needle. And I felt like a human voodoo doll. Everything was painful. But, I reasoned, this was the time to do this terrible chore. If not now, when? No sense schlepping things along with us to a brand new state and then sorting through it there, when our first Christmas in our new house arrived.

What a terrible way to start our new life *that* would be.

Now, as I write, I clearly recall taking all the holiday things out of those old cardboard boxes and repacking them neatly in those big plastic bins. The imported German glass ornaments we bought for one another each year since we first met. The beloved paper Mickey Mouse garland that we bought for our first apartment-sized tree. The tacky Hallmark Star Wars light-up ornaments (and I use the term *ornament* loosely) that Drew's sister had given him a few days after Christmas each year, when they went on sale (yet another inside joke that served to strengthen the familial bond).

And I recall unpacking and repacking our nativity. The crèche that had belonged to my grandmother and of which we had been proud custodians for many years. The one with the conglomeration of composite material holy people, animals, and Gumby-like paper palm trees that were wildly out of proportion. If my memory serves me correctly, there was a cow that could have killed Mary and Joseph just by stepping upon them, much like King Kong. There was also a shepherd who could have taken on all three Wise Men at once and made off with their gifts. No question.

What I don't recall, however, is finding the box containing our precious (sentimentally, if not monetarily) nativity set again after the movers unloaded everything from the two trucks and into our new house in Maine. That was years ago, and we have moved once more since then. Still no trace.

It just disappeared. Vanished. Poof. Gone.

I have spent hours and hours searching for it. I have gone through every box, more than once. Cardboard, plastic, whatever. And, sadly, no sign.

I now view this mysterious loss as an entirely inexplicable and otherworldly event that holds some deeper meaning. It's not unlike when someone in a remote village in Italy calls the Vatican because some wall of their little house is crying tears that form the outline of the Virgin Mary's foot. I consider this a brand of religious miracle on par with the voices that spoke to Joan of Arc before she went into battle, or the linen napkin that reveals the shape of Christ's body in its shroud.

Is it a coincidence that our crèche disappeared at the same time that I was in the depths of despair, relentlessly questioning the meaning of life and God and the tenets of the religion I had grown up believing to be true?

I don't think so.

And, as my journey through grief and the discovery of my true self and the reformulating of my own beliefs continues to unfold, and I begin to regain clarity, I am more and more convinced that "misplacing Jesus" is symbolic of what was going on in my soul. I also know that, one day, He will probably show up again in my life. Just as mysteriously as He disappeared. In fact, I have already seen a few pieces of straw among some Easter ornaments we unpacked this past March, and it looked eerily like the straw from the vintage manger.

HOLY BAGELS

One of the things about Drew's death that has been undeniably positive is the way in which it has freed me from any misplaced guilt I once felt about not getting our family out the door and off to church more frequently.

I remember those stress-filled Sunday mornings, trying not only to get three squirmy, uncooperative, and sleepy children into their flowery frocks and Baby Gap finery but also to make ourselves appear to be superior examples of nurturing, appropriately God-fearing, well-adjusted suburban parents.

Although there were moments of warmth and community as we listened to hymns and participated in what we always jokingly referred to as "Episcopalian aerobics" (kneel, sit, stand, kneel, stand, sit, stand, kneel...rinse, repeat), my memories of religious obedience had more to do for the most part with the promise of some final reward than anything else. That "final reward" being the bagels, doughnuts, and coffee we would procure on our way home from the ten a.m. service. (Another reward was that some of the most lovely sex we ever had was after we'd returned home from church, enjoyed our bagels, and snuck off upstairs, while the kids watched a Winnie the Pooh video.)

So our church excursions were sometimes the sweetest part of the week. But it wasn't about the minister's sermon or the wondrousness of Sunday school. It was eating bagels with our kids and kissing one another after we were back home, with a smidgen of cream cheese still on our lips.

Bagels can, indeed, bring you closer to God.

YES, VIRGINIA...THERE IS AN AFTERLIFE

After Drew was buried in the frozen ground at the local cemetery, and after I'd stopped crying long enough to stop being so pissed off at whatever God there might be, I realized that I wanted to give my children something to grasp on to. I wanted to give them a spiritual base.

I remember the first Easter in our aloneness. It was about three months or so after he died, and I was praying night and day. I didn't know exactly to whom I was praying, but I was begging for help. From anyone who would listen to me.

I sensed that without this spiritual ball and chain, I'd surely float away into the ether, and I'd take my children with me. I wasn't about to let that happen, so I decided to give my children something to hang onto, something to bolster them as they suffered through their own sadness.

Words seemed the way to accomplish this, so I turned to one of the things I loved most: my sizeable collection of vintage children's books. There was one particularly sweet volume from Victorian times that was about Jesus and was apparently a remnant from the Sunday school-teaching days of a woman named Beatrice.

That first spring, I snuggled up with my children in the bed that Drew and I had shared and I read aloud to them the story of Easter. It sounded magical and rather unbelievable, of course, as most religious stories do. But rather than stating it as fact, as a religious "lesson," I asked them what they thought Easter was really all about. What the whole deal was with the stone and the tomb and the dead guy coming back to life. And then, I remember having the most wonderful discussion ever about the meaning of life—with a ten-, seven-, and four-year-old.

It made me smile to hear them using their little brains to think and form their own opinions. This was so different from my own experiences as a child. It felt so refreshingly real and honest, and I found myself liberated, as I shared my own post-widowhood thoughts on life and death with them. Where we thought Drew might be. What he might be up to in the afterlife. And whether there was, indeed, an afterlife.

In the middle of this sweet, touching little talk, it came to me that I could give them all of the spiritual and religious underpinnings they would require—lovingly and meaningfully, simply by all of us spending time together. And by talking with them. And, more importantly, listening to them.

I decided we didn't need a church. We needed the solitude of a forest, with a soft carpet of pine needles underfoot—and a gentle sprinkling of snowflakes. Or maybe the energy of the ocean, with a soft sandy beach to walk upon. Depending upon the season.

Nature became our new religion.

So, although I didn't take my children to church, we became more connected, spiritually, than ever, and I started a wonderfully sweet tradition. Instead of getting all gussied up and going to church on a Sunday morning, we'd put on our comfy warm outdoor clothes and get ready for an adventure.

I'd make hot cocoa for them, coffee for myself, and pack it up in thermoses. We'd grab cups and napkins, and then make a stop at our favorite local bakery to get bagels with cream cheese, and yummy pastry treats. We'd drive a short distance to our favorite conservation land sanctuary and walk through the woods, carrying our backpacks filled with goodies. There were picnic tables in various areas and we'd settle on our favorite, usually one overlooking a small lake. And there we'd sit. In the sunshine, if we were lucky. Or under the clouds. We went there in the snow, when the spring flowers were blooming, and when the beautiful autumn leaves were reflecting in the water and falling in heaps of color all around.

Our discussions were touchingly honest and lovely, but without the innocence that might have been a part had my children not just suffered the loss of their father. That innocence had been stolen from them. And in some ways, from myself, as well.

But the trade-off was this: his death allowed us a new freedom. I would ask them what they believed about things like life and God and death and heaven. And about religion and church. About reincarnation. Even my four-year-old had opinions of his own. And it was wonderful to know that this was my chance to guide them on a journey that was all their own.

In reality, they were teaching me as much or more than I was teaching them.

My children are teenagers now. The only time we've been to church together was for Drew's mother's funeral a few years ago.

It wasn't horrible for them to be in church that day—it's not as if they have some dysfunction that disallows them from walking through a church door.

They don't burst into tears. Or into flames. Their heads don't start spinning around or anything like that.

Church remains, however, a bit of a touchy subject. And they continue to have strong feelings about it. The very first winter after we'd moved to Maine, I remember sitting around the dinner table (back when I more frequently actually had the time and energy to cook dinners) and asking the children if they'd like to think about the possibility of attending a Christmas Eve church service. It had been three years since Drew's holiday season demise, and I thought that perhaps I should make an effort, so I wouldn't remove church from their Christmas memories for all eternity.

Holden, ten at the time, was sitting to the right of me. I vividly recall the conviction in his voice when he said, with watery eyes, "I'm not going to church. You can't make me." The last time he'd visited a church was for his father's funeral. On New Year's Eve. Who could blame him for not wanting to celebrate Christmas there?

And that was the last time I have ever suggested it. I sometimes miss the Christmas hymns and the candlelight, but we make our own magic, in our own meaningful way, and in our special surroundings.

My children all most definitely have their own beliefs. And Drew had a lot to do with that.

In a very real way, he is the one who gave us all new life.

GOD BLESS MAINE

When I moved to Maine, part of the reason was that I knew I needed to be closer to the ocean. To find the inner and outer peace that I would need to heal from the tragedy I'd endured. And I found that peace. I found it in the ocean, and the sand, and in my walks on the beach.

Day after day and night after night. I'd walk and walk and cry and swear and talk to Drew and to the universe and to any other dead relative that might listen. I'd sit on my special perch of rocks, my "mediation rocks," overlooking the sea, and I'd look out at the sun or the moon and feel the spray from the waves crashing below my feet, and I'd ponder. I'd ask *why?* I'd ask *when?* I'd ask *how?*

Ultimately, I'd feel a serenity overtake me that would, at times, make me certain that Drew was watching over me, that he was in the energy of the ocean and the subtle caress of the moonlight on my shoulders. I'd miss him like crazy and I'd cry salty tears into the salty ocean. It made me feel I was part of something far greater than what I could perceive with my own human, limited senses.

When I'd lie in my bed at night, I'd listen to the foghorns and see the lighthouse's beacon shine through the trees in dappled wondrousness. I knew I wasn't alone. The lighthouse became my symbol of hope. The foghorns soothed me to sleep and were my lullaby on nights when I couldn't get his death, or that vast feeling of loneliness, out of my mind.

The coast of Maine has been my spiritual salvation. It's done more for me than any church ever did.

MY LONDON EPIPHANY

Three years or so after Drew died, I took a trip to London. Alone. (See the story in chapter five 5 entitled "The Virgin Suite.") While I was there, I spent countless hours meandering through many museums, and found myself mesmerized by and drawn to all sorts of religious artifacts and artwork. Bits and pieces from ancient altars. Triptychs and diptychs and all manner of gilded wonderfulness.

I apparently already had the stirrings of an idea of what I might be creating, artistically, in the future, and my heart and head seemed to know instinctively what type of inspiration I required.

During a portion of this trip, I happened to be staying at a chic hotel near a venerable Anglican church, St. Martin-in-the-Fields. It was the weekend before Easter and, having been raised Episcopalian, I felt compelled to at least attempt attendance at a Palm Sunday service. It was such a famous church, I just couldn't resist the opportunity to witness the pageantry.

As I sat there, the guy in charge, decked out in an ornate costume, climbed up this two-story curved freestanding staircase to a pulpit in midair. It was from there that he gave his high holiday sermon. I must admit it almost caused me to burst into tears. Not out of sadness, but because it suddenly hit me how oddly disturbing the entire scene was: this man was, almost literally, halfway to heaven, and obviously perched up there at nosebleed height to send a message to us lowly scoundrels down below.

He was just a tad closer to God than we were.

As I listened to his empty words ring in my ears, I thought of my little "sermons" with my children as we ate blueberry muffins on a mossy picnic table overlooking a lake filled with ducks and lily pads, and it finally really hit home: we already had all the spiritual glue we needed.

And I didn't need a trip across the pond to find it.

WHAT IS SACRED?

Since Drew's untimely death (which was very inconvenient and against my direct orders, I might add), I have spent an inordinate number of hours pondering what, indeed, is truly sacred. Perhaps it's because he died at Christmas. I mean, it is difficult to reconcile the death of your soulmate with the simultaneous celebration of the birth of a man whose press release says he is the Son of God. Then you throw Santa Claus and mistletoe into the mix, and you can start to imagine why a woman would need to do some serious pondering about life, love, death, and religion. And what is deemed hallowed or inviolate.

Society holds certain things as sacred. But everything changes when your reality shifts, when you experience an event that propels you out of the ordinary and into the extraordinary, when someone tears up the rules to the game you've been playing since you were born. There is a payoff waiting that you don't expect. You are set free. You think you have been sent to Monopoly jail to serve out a life sentence for a white-collar crime you didn't commit, but instead you have gotten the Get Out of Jail Free card. There is a silver lining.

Being an intimate witness to death does one wonderful thing

for you…it gives you permission not only to buy a new game board but to create your own new rules. Because you have been there. Done that. You know what death is. The horror and the beauty. You're left with something more awe-inspiring than any church sermon. A sacred glimpse, into the unknown. I didn't see Moses with the stone tablet of the Ten Commandments, and I wish I could say I was witness to the whole parting of the Red Sea thing, but I did watch the man I love take his last breath.

That is real for me. That is sacred.

I went through a spiritual transformation, as a partner in Drew's illness and death. I sat in hospital rooms with him and ate seaweed for breakfast (that would have been our macrobiotic diet phase) with him. I suffered with him.

I was pretty sure I would die along with him—but, surprise! I got to hang around afterward and plan the funeral.

Like many people, I have lived through heartbreak and devastation. Like many people, I have prayed and waited for that miracle that never manifested. It has made me reexamine my values, my religious leanings, and my entire belief system. I stood barefoot atop a layer of hot flowing lava for a number of years. I got blisters on my feet. And I'm sure I will always have scars. Only now is that lava cooling and solidifying. Only now do I feel as if I can walk again, without having to worry about falling in and not being able to climb out. Only now am I certain my own passions have not died along with my husband.

Living each day on shaky ground and having no safety net is much like living inside of Aunt Edna's lime green Jell-O mold. The one with tidbits of pineapple and cream cheese in it. Everything looks blurry and is tinted an unnatural color. Every day feels "icky." I don't have an advanced degree in the study of grief and I haven't attended Harvard Divinity School. Although I'm sure they'd love to have me. What I do have is credibility. Because living through death and grief is infinitely more profound than studying it. I am sure I have earned my doctorate a few times over.

And so, after continued pondering, I would like to say that I believe the sacred lies all around us, and within us. The sacred is not something that needs to be in Webster's dictionary. The sacred is intimate and different for each of us. Whether it is worldly objects or memories, we each hold onto that which is sacred to us. We each place it atop our own altar. Be it a bookshelf, a box under our bed next to the dust bunnies, or our mind. We reflect. We remember. We honor and cherish. We cry sacred tears…of pain, and of joy. Sometimes out loud, but most often, in the silence and safety of our own hearts.

While on the topic of the sacred, I have a confession to make. Since being widowed, I have developed a habit that has at times required an intervention.

I love to visit cemeteries. And don't even get me started on old headstones. I love to run my fingers over the words, to study their designs and their beautiful decoration. I long to photograph them. My children have had to endure many stops along many roadsides in many quaint New England towns while mommy snaps photos of lichen-covered pieces of granite.

There's a man in the UK who waited patiently for approximately two hours while I wandered through St. Andrew's, taking photos of the tombstones of dead Scottish people (perhaps that's one of the reasons we never ended up dating and are just friends).

I can't help it. I just have a need to be there. I like to believe Drew has something to do with it. That my appreciation of the world of the dead amongst the living has something to do with him. That the sacred fascinates me because he has become sacred now that he is gone from this earthly existence. Of course, it could also just be some psychological disorder that more than one therapist would be happy to address for me. I think I'd rather just use the money for a hot stone massage and believe that I am evolving into a more spiritually attuned human being.

When you have been close to death, when you no longer fear it, your knowledge of the ephemeral changes. You know that even those headstones won't be here forever, that even those chunks of granite and marble are going to be gone one day. That only our dreams, only our thoughts, only our memories are eternal. The things that seem fleeting are actually the only things that are "real." The only things we can hold on to. The only things we take with us. From childhood to adulthood, from nursery to dorm room to apartment to condo to house to nursing home. They accompany us. Our favorite sweater from our freshman year in college may get lost along the way, but our memory of the boy who let us wear it on that chilly autumn night when we were on our first date doesn't get lost. And if we're fortunate, that sweet memory will accompany us until the day we die. Possibly beyond.

I have a multitude of objects and rituals that are sacred to me. Some live in my mind, some live in the top drawer of my lingerie bureau. Objects that mean as much to me as the cross. The tiny tote bag I carried with me as I boarded the school bus on my first day of kindergarten, my Brownie uniform, my grandmother's breakfast dishes, the first gift my future husband gave me when we were in college, my engagement ring. The list goes on. I am a sentimental saver by nature, so the list actually goes on and on. And on.

(If you are deeply religious, this might be a good time to start praying for me, just in case the following questions are off base and they go on my permanent record, along with the D I got in Algebra 2 my junior year of high school. I'm sure I'll be paying for that for all eternity, also.)

Let me say upfront that I am not suffering from some sort of psychosis. I do not think my husband was the Son of God, and I am not starting my own little cult. But is the death of a loved one less sacred than the death of a man named Jesus?

Does the communion ritual at church on Sunday hold more meaning than our own personally meaningful rituals? Does the champagne I sometimes drink on a Friday evening, in memory of my Friday night champagne ritual with the man I promised my life to, mean less than the silver chalice of (usually bad) red wine? Does the gumball I eat from the vintage gumball machine I gave to Drew when we were first married mean less than the wafers they offer at the church altar?

Happily, for me, the answer right now is *no*.

It's not even that I don't believe in a God. I just don't believe that there is such a chasm between the holy and the everyday. Between a church with a choir singing and a sandy beach with dancing waves crashing. The holy *is* the everyday. We are it. And heaven is, indeed, right here in front of us.

I realize that in sixty years I could be writing a compilation of short stories entitled *Optimistic Essays from Hell,* but I think it is worth the risk. I know that God has a sense of humor, the same way I know that hell, if it does indeed exist, is filled with mini-vans. Humor is a gift. A sacred gift. And, if God does exist, I'm certain He is happy that I'm using His gift to the fullest.

And if He doesn't exist...well then, we'd best just keep laughing.

RINGS ON YOUR FINGERS

The first Thanksgiving after Drew died was not a holiday I was looking toward with joyful anticipation. It marked the advent of the season that would mark the anniversary of his demise. The month between Thanksgiving and Christmas had been a day-by-day journey down the road to the end. And it had all been so ironically accompanied by carols and mistletoe. I was not look-ing forward to living through those memories again.

So I did the only sane thing. I decided to run away from home. I didn't want to be with anyone or around anything that would remind me of the previous year. I invited my mother to join us, and off we went for a three-day visit to a very beautiful inn down on Cape Cod. It was perfect. It was a town we knew well from our summer family vacations, yet it was different, because we had never been there for a winter holiday visit. So it had enough familiarity to make it comforting, but it was a brand new experi-ence for us being there at Thanksgiving.

We stayed in a beautiful little cottage overlooking the ocean, and we walked across the street for a lovely Thanksgiving dinner in the main inn.

The next day, we strolled through the quaint little town center and I stumbled upon a store with a collection of sterling silver rings. In addition to being inexpensive, what I liked was that they had interesting designs on them depicting the ocean. So I bought two nice, silver bands. One had an "ocean wave" design encircling it. The other had a repeating design of various seashells, one next to the other. I didn't hesitate for a minute. I paid for the rings and slipped them both on my finger, one stacked above the other.

I immediately felt a new sense of empowerment and purpose. I had always dreamed of living close to the ocean one day, and I decided that these rings were more than just rings. They were a symbol of my dreams, and of my future. They were to be a visible reminder of the power of the sea, and the power inside of me. I decided to wear them on my left hand…not on the finger that used to be graced by my engagement and wedding rings, but the finger next to it. Close enough to be symbolic. OK, so they are on my left middle finger. Maybe that is also symbolic of some other sentiment I was subconsciously sending out to the universe at large.

They weren't replacing the rings that Drew gave to me when he promised to stay with me forever, but they were just as important. Maybe even more important. They symbolized the tiny shred of faith that still lived somewhere deep inside of my heart. The faith that I would be happy again. Truly happy. And fulfilled. The faith that the tears would stop falling on a daily basis. That my heart would stop aching. That I would be able to breathe again. And that I could look at a photo of Drew without feeling as if I wanted to die, too.

I made a conscious decision right at that moment to wear those rings day and night, as a symbol of my heart's desire and a reminder that there were still things in life that filled me with excitement, happiness, and wonder.

The week after returning, I met a friend for breakfast and then we did some shopping. I was browsing in a little shop when I found one more silver band. This time, it had tiny stars, hearts, and a moon engraved on it, along with *magic* written in a charming script. I knew I was meant to have found it. I slipped it on so it rested above the other two. It was perfect.

That was Thanksgiving of 2003. Today, I still wear those three rings. I think I can count the number of times I have taken them off. I've been complimented on them often and have grown accustomed to telling people the lovely little story of how I found them and why I wear them.

I no longer just dream of living near the ocean. I see a tiny sliver of it from the magical porch of my beautiful 1920s-era house in Maine. I can also see it as I lie in bed at night. Well, at least in the wintertime, when the leaves are off the trees. I have no doubt that, had it not been for the faith those rings inspired—faith in myself, faith that I had something better than just grief waiting for me—I would have never made it to where I am today. To the ocean.

So follow your heart. And listen to that tiny, barely audible voice inside you. It is trying to tell you something important. Something that could lead you to the places and people you only dream of.

11
MONEY

DEATH HAS A WAY of sucking the fun out of money.

When you go through any type of trauma where money becomes a kind of consolation prize, you are in for one doozy of a learning experience.

I buried my husband, and a few short weeks later, thanks to something called life insurance, I had the thing we'd always wished we'd had when we were married: a bank account full of cold, hard cash. And that's a good description for it. Cold. And hard.

Suddenly, I had money. I wasn't a gazillionaire. Or even a millionaire. But still, I knew I could spend time cobbling my life back together and take my time healing and being a mother to my grieving children, rather than rushing off to take the first decent paying job in an attempt to pay the gas bill.

Although this appeared to be a blessing initially, it turned out to be both a blessing and a curse. Here's why: Had I been forced to rush full-steam ahead and join the nine-to-five workforce for the sole purpose of paying the mortgage and avoiding foreclosure, I would have been provided with a very convenient way to keep myself numb. I'd have been running around in a tizzy, ping-ponging from work to taking care of my kids to maintaining a house and a semblance of a life. And the entire time, I'd have been worrying whether our children were being caused yet more damage by being relegated to days spent in childcare, while still in an extremely fragile state...mourning the loss of their daddy. I would have collapsed into my bed each evening, physically exhausted, emotionally spent, and guilt-ridden, and gotten up each morning to repeat the same procedure.

In the words of Pink Floyd, I would have become "comfortably numb."

Isn't this the way much of the American public spend their lives? Isn't it the way we are conditioned to exist? In a state of numbness. The hamster wheel way of life. And if all of the jobs, hobbies, chores, commitments, and volunteer duties aren't enough to wear people out and keep them from feeling their true feelings, or painful inner discontent, there are always drugs or alcohol to finish the job. We exhaust ourselves so we have enough money to buy the things we might or might not actually need, to achieve that elusive thing called "happiness."

But I had found out what true happiness was, and it wasn't attached to a dollar sign.

So, instead of being forced into the nine-to-five routine, and having my thoughts and body occupied twenty-four hours a day, I was very kindly handed option number two. I was able to stay at home, take my time, decide what my next steps would be as I climbed up out of my own personal hell, and be present for my young children.

THE ART OF MAKING MONEY

I went to an art college. That's where I met Drew. He was a film major, I was an illustration major. We had a romance and a life together steeped in creativity. But, although I'm an artist, I've never been fond of the whole "starving artist" notion, and I consider commercial art a beautiful thing. So let's get one thing straight: I do like to make money, and although I am very much in favor of helping others, I consider capitalism to be a worthy lifestyle. I've never been a fan of socialism or communism. I was fortunate enough to be born a citizen of the good old U S of A, and I'm good going along with the plan for the most part. Not because I desire five sailboats and three vacation homes, but because I am convinced that the making of money affords one the opportunity to do more good in the world than would be possible otherwise. That's just the way it goes. As a wise and very successful business acquaintance once said to me, "Bill Gates will do more good for humanity than most of the nonprofits in the world added together."

Having dealt with a number of nonprofits in my post-widow-hood career, and having witnessed the red tape, zero budgets, and frequent ridiculousness that goes on behind their closed doors, even in light of their usually very good and heartfelt intentions, I do tend to agree with him.

Of course, I'll need to eat my words if and when I ever start a nonprofit of my own, but I'm willing to take that risk.

Now although I have always believed that making money is important because it gives one freedom, I haven't always been very confident in my God-given ability to do so. I had jobs as a teenager and I worked in and out of college, but I hadn't spent many years supporting myself fully.

I lacked confidence in myself in that way. At one point in my adult life, self-analysis helped me come to the realization that this lack of money-making confidence could all be traced back to a comment my father made to me one day during my early teenage years, when my parents were in the midst of an ulcer-inducing divorce.

I was cleaning his office on a Saturday, during one of our rather strained, semi-monthly weekend visits. It was his little way of providing me an opportunity to make some cash, while also getting his workspace tidied up. I imagine I was moving too slowly, or hadn't dusted behind the plant or some such thing and, as was his perfectionistic habit, he chose to dwell on my flaws rather than my strengths, making the off-handed judgment that I was just like my mother. An inability to step up to the plate, work hard, and contribute when it was truly needed was suggested. A weakness was implied. And although I don't for a minute believe it was true of my mother, it was his opinion and he chose that moment to share it with me. I didn't grasp the impact until decades later when I had children of my own, and realized how careless parental comments can affect a child and his or her self-esteem at its very core.

I'm not sure any decent therapist would place the entire blame for this unfounded insecurity on my now long-deceased father, but the bottom line is I've always had money issues. And my greatest fear as an adult was that I would be a failure at supporting my family should I need to. That I couldn't be the breadwinner. Didn't have it in me. Wasn't capable enough.

So naturally, to aid me in addressing this issue, the universe or God or whatever force is in charge sat back one day and thought, *Hmmmm. This one really needs some help. Let's see what happens if we take her husband away from her so she not only has to grieve the loss of his love but also the loss of his biweekly paychecks. Ha! That should teach her a lesson or two.*

My worst nightmare had come to fruition. Well actually, two of my worst nightmares: I'd lost my husband, and I'd need to figure out how to support myself and my children, completely on my own.

Before I had children, I had first been employed as a freelance graphic designer, then as a full-time graphic designer at a public relations company, and finally started a business of my own, designing and creating artistic, upscale, handmade invitations for special events in both the private and corporate sectors. Admittedly, it was not always a successful business in the dollar-sign sense, but I had something that I worked at each day. I had a dream I was living, plans I was making. I also, luckily, had a husband who supported me emotionally and creatively as well as, often, monetarily. We were a team. All of our money went into the same pot at the end of the day. That's the way we wanted it.

When our three children were born, I kept working as much as was humanly possible. With baby number two, I moved my business out of the space I'd been renting nearby and into our house. Like many women, I tried to balance work, motherhood, and marriage. Drew and I had always agreed that we wanted one of us to be at home to raise our own children. Or to always remain in careers that allowed us to take turns being present. It was a topic that never even needed to come up for discussion because we knew we both felt the same way. We used the occasional preschool for a temporary respite from full-time parenting, but I was basically a stay-at-home mom. And therefore, my business was stay-at-home, too.

When Drew was diagnosed with cancer, our youngest son, Cole, was barely one-and-a-half. We decided then and there that something was going to have to go, and that something was my work.

Nothing mattered but taking care of Drew and maintaining a semblance of a semi-normal family life, for the sake of our children, and ourselves.

Suddenly, money didn't matter. We'd just about finished the do-it-mostly-ourselves six-year restoration of our home, and our bank account was pretty much drained, but Drew had very good health insurance so we knew we could survive.

A year after his surgery for pancreatic cancer, his employer laid him off. Having spent most of his adult life as a freelancer in the film industry, and with occasional stints in managerial positions at film industry–related businesses in which he was financially vested, he had taken a job as a producer at a local company around the time our third child was born. Although we had both always enjoyed the flexibility and spontaneity that came with the freelance lifestyle, having three children made us more aware of the benefits of a nine-to-five job. At least for a while.

Although I was hard pressed to feel anything positive toward a company that could lay off a man with terminal cancer and three children to support, I tried to view it as some brand of a blessing—a chance for us to scoop up our kids and have an adventure. Maybe move to California, so Drew could stretch his filmmaking wings. Physically, he was doing very well and, suddenly, the chance to do whatever we wanted to do or to go wherever the wind might take us felt very right and quite appealing.

Drew's male ego, however, did not view this as an opportunity for adventure; he saw it as being rejected in the worst way possible. This frustrated me to some degree, but I wasn't about to force the issue. I thought we already had enough stress in our life. I just found it nearly impossible to understand how he could have what had been labeled a "terminal" cancer, yet still be afraid to break the rules and take a chance at a new life. We clearly had very different risk tolerance levels. I'm sure at the time, part of me thought that maybe, just maybe, if we ran all the way to the other side of the continent, his cancer wouldn't be able to find us. Maybe if we no longer had to go in for checkups at the place where his tumor had first been discovered, it would all just disappear.

At the time, I would have happily sold everything and hopped on a plane with my husband and our three children and started a new life. I wanted to dream again, to hope again, and to live again, without the shadow of cancer over our lives.

I'M GONNA WASH THAT MONEY
RIGHT OUTTA MY HAIR

The funny part is, deep in my soul, I think I've always wanted to get rid of the money that was a direct result of Drew's death. Most people wouldn't understand unless, perhaps, they've acquired money as a result of widowhood, or an accident, or some other type of devastating loss. Money represents energy. It needs to keep moving, to be given and taken freely in order to keep the cosmic flow going. It's like blood. It's like a winding river. And although we all deserve to receive money for the energy we expend, and although we all deserve to be paid for our talents and for our hard work, money that comes to you because of a negative event is not money with good energy; it's dirty money.

It's tainted. You have it, you need it, but you don't really want it. You feel you deserve it, but it doesn't make you feel happy. It doesn't make you feel joyful.

Instead, it is a painful reminder of what you've lost. It also contains a bit of guilt-inducing magic, because here is this money that represents your beloved husband's death...and life...and my God, you'd better do something good with it. You'd better not waste it. Or squander it. You'd better use it in a smart way, and you'd better not end up destitute and homeless down the road, with your three children in tow because, really, what would your deceased husband, or your Aunt Eleanor, think of *that*?

Talk about pressure. Talk about feeling as if you're under a microscope.

I've had all kinds of reactions to my widow-with-a-bit-of-money situation. I've had some men (they're almost always men) treat me as if I cannot take care of myself. They've jokingly said things like, "Oh, you're dating a doctor? You'd better hang onto him!" Or, "Just don't spend it all and end up like my mother-in-law. After her divorce, she blew it all, and now look at her." I once had a financial advisor who made it perfectly clear that I'd best hang onto this cash or else find a wealthy new husband.

Gee, thanks for the vote of confidence.

What I've always thought was this: I've been dealt a really crappy hand and I'm going to spend as much time raising my children, sans a childcare provider, as possible. I'm going to use this money to afford us time together. I'm going to use this money to take them places and experience things together. I'm going to live like I could drop dead tomorrow. Or like they could. I'm not going to buy into the American dream and work nine-to-five while a nanny raises them, only to later retire and wonder where my life went and why my children and I barely know one another.

Drew and I never wanted that kind of life. And now that I was alone, I still didn't.

The difference was, now I had some extra money to really live "the dream." Only he wasn't with me anymore, so it wasn't really much of a dream.

It felt like more a nightmare…albeit, a well-funded one.

DING-DONG—YOUR FUTURE FORECLOSURE IS CALLING

I remember the financial planning guy arriving at my door a month or so after Drew had died. He was the brother of one of

Drew's good friends, and I both liked and trusted him. After we talked extensively and after he had collected the requisite data, he went back to his office to run some numbers and write up a "plan" for my financial future.

When he returned shortly thereafter, I sat across from him at my dining room table, in the chair where Drew had sat for our last Thanksgiving dinner only a couple of months earlier. He flipped through the pages of his notebook containing charts and graphs in a rainbow of colors, and as he showed me a "bottom line" of figures, I quickly did some mental calculations before declaring aloud, "So, theoretically, we could live off of this for ten years before I'd have to worry about money."

Then he looked me in the eyes, chuckled and said, "But of course you wouldn't want to do that." I stood with the beginnings of a sad, silent widowed smile upon my lips and thought to myself, *You bet your ass I would.*

And I did. The rest, as they say, is history. (I'm sorry Mr. Financial Advisor, but I was a bad, bad girl.)

It's not that I was lazy. It's just that I felt dead. I can't explain it in any other way. I didn't care if I lived another day. But I had children, so I had to care. I felt as if the most important thing in my life had been stolen from me, and some money to live off of was the least this crappy and unfair universe of ours could do for me and my children. Not only was he gone, but the creative energy that used to drive my dreams and ambitions was MIA too. Life sucked, and I saw no reason to save money from my husband's death so I could travel to Europe in my golden years.

The last thing I want to be doing thirty years after Drew's demise is buying a plane ticket with money from his life insurance policy. Talk about bad karma. Talk about hanging onto the past. I'd rather live in a tent than do that. And I think you might be able to guess how much I dislike camping.

So approximately nine-and-a-half years later, my savings have dwindled. My financial advisors have not always had much faith in me, with some reason (although, with my book and other creative projects finally coming to fruition, and with media coverage providing me credibility, that seems to be changing). Admittedly, I have spent money on vacations with my kids that some people would have spent on a new roof. Or would have socked away in some IRA. Yes, I've invested in braces and guitar lessons and the school ski club and family dinners at our favorite sushi restaurant more often than was probably advisable.

But you know what? My firstborn is now away at college and I wouldn't have missed one day that I've had with her. Not one overpriced sushi dinner. Not one night in a fancy hotel on our minivan road trips. And the closer I get to using up Drew's life insurance money, the more buoyant and blessed I feel. Sure, it's a bit stressful, knowing that one day soon I'll need to be relying totally on my own devices. Without life insurance money from my dead husband or a secondary income from a new partner.

Without much of a safety net.

But in addition to being a bit scary and nerve-wracking, it's also more than a bit exciting. I'm starting a new life. Finally. And instead of a constant in my daily consciousness, Drew will be a wonderful memory in my heart. And every time I open my bank statement, or see my financial advisor, I won't feel sad because it reminds me of his death or guilty because I'm wondering whether I spent that money in a way Drew would have approved.

I know it sounds crazy because, really, people usually try like hell to hold onto their money. But holding onto things doesn't make them yours. It doesn't make them stay. It's a false security. Whether it's money or people or possessions. Things leave us. The only true constant in life is change.

Since Drew's death, whenever I get scared I think, "What's the worst thing that could happen?" If the answer isn't "cancer," it's nothing that bad.

I now know that money is fluid. It can provide things, but really, it's merely freedom. Freedom to choose to do what you want. And Drew gave me that gift. His death imprisoned me in some ways, but the money he left me with set me free to heal, to explore, and to expand upon the "me" I discovered when I finally found myself again. It allowed me to stretch my creative wings, to leave my comfort zone, to search for ways to help others, and to go into the world and create the life and the career I've dreamed of. It set me free to dig deeply into my soul, instead of filling my days with work that paid the bills but didn't heal my heart.

In his life, Drew always supported my dreams…and in a big way, he still does.

In a practical manner, the money I received upon his death provided a cushion. Not a windfall that meant we'd never again have to worry about anything, but something to tide us over and to give our children and myself time to heal—together. But more than that, it's the memory of his love for me that enabled me to accomplish what I have. The victories and the achievements are always a little bittersweet, however, because all I want is to run home to him, to call him on the phone, to have a bottle of champagne to share with our dinner, to tell him my "exciting news."

Instead, I do those things with him in the silence of my dreams and prayers, and I thank the powers that be for all of the good in my life, for the opportunity to follow my heart, and for the man whose smile and laughter continue to inspire my success in life, even in his death.

"WOW, MOM! I'M SO PROUD OF YOU!"

"So…are we making any money yet?"

This quote from the then twelve-year-old Holden, really doesn't require much in the way of an explanation. Suffice it to say that he has always been the most outspoken of my three children, and probably the most tuned in to the universe and the flow of life in general. As his mother, I've always suspected that he's a two thousand-year-old soul, currently trapped in an adolescent body in the throes of hormonal mutiny. I am praying he doesn't lose all of that old soul wisdom in the heat of battle. He also happens to be, unfortunately for his closest friends and family, a Sagittarius. Which, according to my astrological research, means that he has a refreshingly charming way of complimenting people, while simultaneously insulting them. Even I, as his loving mother and someone who is not all that big into the astrology thing, have to admit this to be accurate.

Holden, I love you. Thanks for your vote of confidence. Don't worry, I'm going to make sure they don't repossess the house and that you can go away to college one day.

And I promise you will still always be proud of me.

PEDICURES AND PUBLIC SPEAKING

So just to be clear, although I've had a cushion of life insurance funding and although I've chosen to spend as much time as a stay-at-home mom as possible, it's not as if I've merely been eating bonbons and getting my toenails painted since Drew's death.

I've been working like crazy—but only on the things that bring meaning to my life, into my children's lives, and hopefully, into the lives of others. I've been operating on pure faith that all of my hard work and dedication to my various creative "projects" will eventually come together. And I think I've finally realized that if they don't, hey, at least when I die and my children get *my* life insurance money, they'll know that I had no regrets. I did what I needed to do. I followed my dreams and pursued the work that truly called to me…from the depths of my soul.

Within the first five months of Drew's death, I recall a moment of distinct enlightenment. I had a vision, a waking dream, and in it I saw pieces of artwork I had made, mounted on the pristine white walls of a gallery on Newbury Street in Boston. For those of you unfamiliar with Boston, it is the chic street where the trendiest galleries are tucked away. And beside each piece of artwork was a corresponding story I had written, neatly displayed. It was all very calm, serene, and minimalist in tone.

Now, at that stage in my widowhood, but for journal entries I had been scribbling through my tears at night, I hadn't written anything with any creative intent behind it. Nor had I so much as given a single thought to making any art. In fact, all of my creativity was locked away somewhere dark and dank, along with my heart.

So it was a huge surprise when I suddenly knew what my future held: I was supposed to be writing. And speaking. In front of people. Lots of people.

And I was supposed to be communicating—using both my words and my visual artistic talents.

The next day, I called one of Drew's good friends to get a dose of the testosterone connection I had so often missed since his death, and during that conversation, I excitedly shared with him my vision. My calling. My enlightenment.

He was a dear friend and usually nothing but supportive, but when I mentioned the public speaking thing, even he was a bit shocked. In fact, I distinctly remember a pause on the other end of the phone, and then his words in my ear: "Really? That's just about the last thing I'd ever imagine you doing, Sandi."

His reaction didn't upset me, probably because it mirrored my own feelings of shock at this turn of events. Me? Public speaking? Who the hell could have come up with this crazy idea? Me? The woman who was once so shy in high school that she ate the core of an apple, including the seeds, just to avoid walking to the trash can in front of a cafeteria filled with peers? Me? The woman whose stomach would do flip-flops while doing a Sunday morning Bible reading before a congregation of a whopping thirty-six people? Most of whom probably required a hearing aid and wouldn't have had the foggiest notion whether or not I was pronouncing any of those biblical guys' names correctly anyway.

They say when you feel compelled to do something even though it makes absolutely zero sense, then you are on the right path. Well, this was my lightning bolt. My express train. And I knew I had no choice but to climb on board and surrender to the greater wisdom of the universe.

I was filled with anticipation. I was also pretty sure I needed an antacid.

I have felt blessed to have always been a creative person—someone who could use that creativity as a way to express my grief and to reach out to and connect with others.

I am doing things I never dreamed of doing until I lost Drew. My dreams changed in a heartbeat. And somehow, those dreams are all coming to fruition.

For instance, in spite of the fact that I never aspired to be a writer, I am now a writer. I never dreamed of having a newspaper column. And now, I have a bi-weekly newspaper column. And I adore it. I've penned enough short stories and essays to fill many books. I've designed and launched various projects that celebrate fearlessness, rebelliousness, and, most importantly, the ability to find humor in the face of life's challenges, no matter how overwhelming they might appear.

I've created The Irreverent Widow—a project based upon my experiences, my writing, and on an original exhibit of my own art and words by the same name—that has grown into the larger vision of a social movement and a touring, community-based exhibit designed to help others grieve. And parts of this project are creatively funded, because of my strong belief that *people shouldn't have to pay to grieve*. I've also created a networking project called Girl Scout Dropout (GSD, for short): an online and real-life community where like-minded women (and some brave men) can celebrate their fun, fearless way of living, embrace their rebellious spirits, and support one another with strength and humor through life's challenges. And purchase many of the well-deserved (but definitely not Girl Scout sanctioned) badges earned along the way—because I believe we all need more recognition.

I've been able to accomplish what I've accomplished in my creative life because I've felt absolutely compelled to do these things. I've had no choice. I've been able to be philanthropic because I wasn't doing it for the money; I was doing it so that I could heal. So that my family could heal.

I chose not to lock Drew's life insurance money away and save it for my retirement. I chose to use it to live in the here and now, and to trust that as long as I'm moving forward with my dreams and keep putting forth my best effort, the "future" will take care of itself.

CHRISTMAS IN JULY

Interstate relocation with three kids, two cats, a fish, and a dwarf hamster

When I had finally made up my mind to not only move, but to move to Maine, I couldn't start packing fast enough. I found a buyer for our charming little house in the woods and then began an immediate quest for as much corrugated cardboard, in the form of boxes, as possible. I wrangled them from grocery stores, liquor stores, any store, anywhere. This wasn't a job for those big, relatively expensive plastic storage containers; this was *Moving*, and we needed hundreds and hundreds of cheap boxes if we were going to bring our houseful of stuff along with us to Maine and still have enough money left to pay the movers.

"I'd like one bottle of sauvignon blanc...oh, and do you really need the three dozen cardboard boxes back there in your storage room?"

I bought boxes. I stole boxes. I begged for boxes. I was shameless in my pursuit of corrugated cardboard. Packing paper was my friend. And don't even get me started on that brown sticky tape. I had a collection of three different styles of dispensers—and each caused me a new level of pain and suffering. I don't know what type of education or advanced training the people who invented those packing tape dispensers possessed, but they were not brain surgeons. And they clearly did not hold degrees in either engineering or industrial design.

I did the bulk of the packing myself (with the occasional aid of my always helpful mother), and by D-day (or M-day), I was spent. I'd moved before. I had even moved with three children (and pets) in the mix. And without bragging, I can say in all good conscience that I'd become quite an expert packer. But I'd never moved without Drew. And I'd never packed up an entire household while simultaneously grieving the loss of a husband.

If there is a hell, I imagine this would be one of the torments you'd be subjected to. Moving and packing are stressful under any conditions, even if you're moving for happy reasons. But grieving, packing, and moving most definitely do not mix.

With this in mind, it is clearly no coincidence that the day the movers packed up the last box of pots and pans and loaded the last silver-plated fork onto the moving van was the twenty-fifth day of the seventh month of the Christian calendar.

Christmas in July.

Now, I always thought this ridiculousness was a retail-marketing ploy, but after further investigation, this is what I discovered: According to a source which I have long forgotten, Christmas in July imitates the festivities of the actual Christmas and signifies our yearning for the coolness of winter amid the scorching summer months.

Apparently, people everywhere are sipping frosty cold eggnog and caroling together in the glow of an air conditioner. I had no idea. My limited experience with "Christmas in July" is this: in the summer of 2005, I watched as a handful of compactly built men, speaking in a Slavic tongue, placed the contents of my family's life into a moving van pointed northward, towards Maine. I remember hearing Christmas carols emanating from the tiny radio in the newly barren kitchen, as they packed up the last of the good china. At first I thought I was hallucinating, but as José Feliciano belted out "Feliz Navidad," I realized it was July 25th. Christmas in July. And there we were, moving out of the house where my husband had died, over two years before, on the morning after Christmas.

The irony was not lost on me. In fact, it was comfortingly disturbing.

As I watched the two moving vans drive off, and as I strategically filled our already filled-to-the-brim Ford Explorer with my three children, our two cats, fish, and a dwarf hamster, I felt certain that north was the right direction to be heading. A new world of possibilities seemed to be laid out before us. Had I not been so exhausted, I surely would have been crying, closing the door for the final time on the life that never came to be. Sometimes, you grieve what *could have been* even more deeply than the memories of what you did have.

We were keeping Drew in our hearts, but leaving his bones in a cemetery in Massachusetts, as we moved on to begin a new life in Maine. And as we pulled out of our driveway and the sweet and familiar crunch of the gravel rang in my ears one last time, I knew we were doing the right thing.

12
ENDINGS AND BEGINNINGS

EVERYONE WANTS a happy ending.

The handsome prince tears into town on his white stallion, or hot BMW motorcycle, and sweeps the boyfriendless widow off of her vintage cowboy–booted feet.

The guy who just moved into the house next door turns out to be the man of her dreams.

Her husband didn't actually die: the doctors at Dana-Farber had his body cryogenically frozen, have subsequently come up with the cure for his previously terminal cancer, and he walks back in through the kitchen door one Halloween Eve while she's carving pumpkins with their three children and mulling cider.

That's what people want to hear.

But, alas, that's not quite what I have to report, nine years and eight months down the long and winding widowhood road.

Admittedly, I've had some close calls that would have made quite the romantic ending to this first book of mine. All are interesting but, interestingly, none have worked out quite as imagined.

And so, that said, I respectfully submit to you the following real-life reports.

Perfect Ending 1

College déjà vu

When my daughter, Olivia, thought that she wanted to attend The University of the Arts (formerly known as the Philadelphia College of Art) where her dad and I met, the place where we first laid eyes upon one another, the place where we fell madly and deeply and forever-after in love, I thought, *Wow. This could be four years of emotional hell and will result in incredible debt, but what a perfect ending for my book!*

The blatantly dramatic city college backdrop, paired with the heart-wrenching memories of our young courtship, held the potential for four long years filled with endless Hallmark movie-of-the-week moments. I could have spent forty-eight months in tears. Or having flashbacks. Probably in conjunction with the hot flashes that my currently menopausal friends swear will be arriving at my doorstep at any moment.

But although it came down to the wire, in the end Olivia decided not to attend the college where Drew and I met. And my emotional torment was limited to just two exploratory college visits to our old stomping ground during her senior year of high school.

At one point during our second pilgrimage to my alma mater, while I sat on a set of steps across from an open classroom door listening to her chatting away animatedly with some film students, I glanced up and I noticed a dinosaurish piece of editing equipment, in a very familiar shade of iridescent, 1960s stratosphere blue. It was the iconic Steenbeck, the same editing machine Drew could often be found hunched over, splicing together a project for one of his film classes, when we were in the throes of early romance. As the image and the name soaked in, I could see him sitting there, turning his handsome head and smiling at me with his Ultra Brite teeth and warm brown eyes, and was immediately transported back to the early 1980s. The sweet, salty tangle of emotion made me dizzy. I wondered how I would possibly make it through four years of such raw yet wondrous memories.

Fortunately, I didn't have to.

Olivia is now happily matriculated at the equally prestigious and substantially less sentimentally significant Massachusetts College of Art & Design, in Boston. OK, so it's located around the corner from the very same hospitals where Drew went through his pancreatic cancer drama, but at least it's not the same place where we first made love, or kissed one another in the photography darkroom, or penned forbidden flirtations to one another in English class. The feelings associated with her current locale are a bit different. They are associated with the end, rather than the beginning. And somehow, the beginning, with all of its unfinished dreams, can be more difficult, at times, to relive.

Say good-bye to perfect ending 1.

Perfect Ending 2

The man who awoke from his coma on my wedding day

In March of 2011, as I was in the final throes of college-decision-making mania with Olivia, I stumbled upon a fascinating man who turned out to be what my editor, myself, and a number of my close friends considered to be the potential "perfect ending."

Our meeting is a testament to the amazing ways in which a social media tool such as Facebook can connect two people who, in real life, wouldn't have had a snowball's chance in hell of meeting.

I had made a comment on the Facebook page of a common acquaintance, and this man read it, apparently thought I was interesting, checked out who I was in cyberspace, and soon thereafter, posted a comment in reaction to something I had written on my own Facebook page. I don't remember his exact words, but I picked up on a hint of possible sarcasm, and being a lover of well-executed sarcastic wit, felt compelled to see who this wise-ass guy was.

When I found out, I was floored. End of story. Or rather, beginning of story.

Having suffered a horribly dramatic fall while in his mid-twenties, which resulted in a traumatic brain injury, he had awakened from his twelve-day-long coma in a hospital in Boston on the 8th of October, 1988. My wedding day.

We began a lengthy exchange of communication, both written and telephonic. Long conversations that lasted far too long into the night, especially when it was a school night.

I really liked him. A lot.

In my soul, I'd always felt that, were I ever to find the new perfect man for me, he'd need to have suffered to the extent I felt I'd suffered. He'd need to be "damaged" to the degree I felt I had been, in order to truly understand the depth of my heartache. Of course, this situation took that belief a bit further than was probably advisable.

Still, I thought, *Wow. This could be an interesting relationship. I've never dated a man with clinically diagnosed bipolar disorder, PTSD, hypoglycemia, and a brain injury. But he seems more "normal" than some of the other men I've dated, has amazing emotional depth, is wonderfully sweet and loving, and he woke up on my wedding day. This could not only be an adventure, but the perfect ending for my book!*

Usually—and sometimes to my own detriment—I tend not to take the "labels" put upon people too seriously. I like to form my own opinions.

A creative person by both trade and passion, he had written poetry, songs, and a play that told his dramatic story, all with optimism for the future. He was witty, engaging, and also a certain and very appealing brand of brilliant. Having weathered my own drama, and having used the experience to write stories and create an art exhibit intended to help myself and others to heal, I felt an instant and very personal connection to his work, his journey, and his ability to inject humor into a situation that would have caused lesser human beings to curl up and hide under their covers for the rest of their lives.

I admired his strength and understood his longing for that which he had lost. And I respected him more than any other man I'd *known* since Drew's death, much less dated.

Unfortunately, although the quasi-fairy tale seemed feasible on paper, reality wasn't quite so simple. I had forgotten that no matter what one's outward appearance, a traumatic brain injury does indeed manifest in real-life challenges and problems. In the end, they were simply too large for me to deal with. Bipolar disorder on its own would have been enough to cause relationship difficulties, even under the best of circumstances, but a brain injury of the type he sustained often results in many lingering consequences.

I was often confounded by his behavior, until I realized that it wasn't his fault. And although I could rationally understand many of the facts of brain injury, I didn't love him enough to want to make it part of my life. I felt as if I deserved to be on dating easy street, not on another road with yet more potholes. Deep ones. No matter how adoring and kind-hearted he was.

I thank him for cracking open my heart and my mind, and for being the catalyst that helped me to feel true compassion once again. But my love for him wasn't unconditional. And as much as I oh-so-wanted it to be my perfect ending, for both personal and professional reasons, it was not meant to be.

So that's it for perfect ending 2.

Perfect Ending 3

Mr. Illustration

Approximately five short weeks after I had put the brakes on things with Mr. Perfect Ending 2, I received an email from a lovely-sounding gentleman who wished to explore the possibility of using my talents to illustrate some books. Not just one, but possibly a whole bunch. As I read his email on my iPhone while standing in line with my two older children, waiting for a table in the sunlit café of a Boston museum, a smile of major proportion appeared upon my face. I had been doing nothing but writing stories and formulating a variety of business plans for what felt like an eternity, and my inside lit up at the prospect of making some art again.

Finally! Art!

Not thinking of him as anything other than a possible collaborative work prospect, I envisioned him as a height-challenged, divorced gentleman with a paunchy tummy overhanging his ill-fitting slacks and possibly a bad comb-over. Admittedly, this rather unattractive image aided in deterring me from tossing aside other commitments to make room in my schedule for an in-person meeting. So the summer rolled by and the sand on my flip-flops accumulated while he patiently persisted in his attempts to meet up with me. To review my portfolio.

When I finally succumbed to the gentle pressure and met with him in early September, I wondered why I hadn't agreed to meet him the very moment he'd emailed me back in July.

One glance at his face and something somewhere inside me thought, *perfect ending.* And just in the nick of time—because, gee, I'd just finished chapter ten, and I only had one more chapter to write before *The End.*

And I needed a kick-ass one!

It turned out, he wasn't divorced, wasn't paunchy, and did not have a bad comb-over. Or any comb-over. He had real hair. The kind I could happily run my fingers through. For hours.

He was actually quite cute. Not to mention six-foot-one. My ultimate upward-head-tilt "perfect guy" kissing height.

Do you know when there is an image of the perfect man burned into your subconscious, at a level so deep that when you see him, you feel as if you've always been waking up naked next to him? Well, that was this guy. Right down to the precise length of his slightly wavy, irresistibly unkempt hair, and the way his eyes twinkled with both sarcasm and childlike happiness when he smiled at me. A combination of the only boy I ever played hooky with in high school and the first boy I French-kissed at a summer church camp in the eighth grade, he touched something wonderful in the recesses of my memory.

The words he wrote, the things he valued, and the thoughts he shared with me spoke to my heart on the deepest of levels. I would have illustrated anything for him any day of the week. Clothing was optional. And when I woke up and glanced at him lying beside me late one evening (something I could have predicted happening from the very moment I found out he had hair), a tiny voice inside of me thought, *Wow.*

Admittedly, it's one of the very few times I've had that reaction to anyone since the first time Drew fell asleep on my bed beside me, fully clothed, on my first day back in Philadelphia during our junior year of college. It was late August of 1981, and I woke up next to him as he lay there still asleep, in his khaki button-down military-style shirt, sultry summer tan, and thick, dark, wavy hair. With the sun just beginning to peek in through my bedroom windows, I looked over at him and the only word that came to mind was, *Wow.*

You don't meet many "wows" in one lifetime. Or at least men who are wows not only on the outside but on the inside, where it truly counts.

Mr. Illustration and I had some sort of interesting little thing going on. I imagine it may have ultimately involved actual creative collaboration, it may have involved friendship, it may indeed have continued to involve nudity, or merely lessons we were karmically meant to teach one another. All I know is, it was a whole lot of fun to be the recipient of a *pleasant* surprise from the universe.

Unfortunately, certain issues got in the way of Mr. Illustration and I having the brand of romantic relationship for which I'd spent a good portion of the last decade of my life searching. For example, while I am apparently on the precipice of being added to AARP's mailing list (who knew?!), he continued to delude himself into thinking he was closer to the age of a college frat boy than to people with enough birthdays under their belt to receive complimentary discounts on their Astroglide.

Also, I have the responsibilities that come with being the mother to three children, and have trouble sometimes leaving the house for a required medical procedure. Whereas he reveled in his ability to come and go as he pleased. Awesome! He liked to camp; I am a proud Girl Scout Dropout. He was allergic to cats; I consider the cat to be the perfect pet, and generally have two in my home at all times. I have the ability to stay up until all hours of the night; he went to bed earlier than my seventy-five-year-old mother. My life is an open book; his was locked up in a leather satchel. And he seemed to prefer it that way.

Of course, there was also the fact that he was emotionally unavailable, and in love with his large (but sweet) dog. And we all know how much I adore men who have primary relationships with their dogs.

There are usually viable reasons why a man can be tall, dark, and handsome and have reached his fifth decade of life without having been snatched up.

Auf Wiedersehen to perfect ending 3. It would clearly never work.

And that's OK, because the anti-Prince Charming version of Mr. Illustration was infinitely more interesting than the classic fairytale-ending hero. Undoubtedly, the story would have gone south when our dwarf Belgian bunny, Boomer, was eaten by his large dog, when his perfectly touchable and disheveled brown hair started falling out in three years, and when at some point he moved into a yurt.

I mean, clearly, a real princess couldn't be running her various creative businesses from a yurt somewhere in the Enchanted Forest.

So, although Mr. Illustration has not provided me with the magical ending those of us who grew up reading fairytales may have been rooting for, he did provide me with laughter, stimulation (intellectual and otherwise), and an abundance of creative and emotional challenges…as well as continued fodder and food for thought. He opened my heart and my mind a few notches further, enabled me to feel more vulnerable, more compassionate, and infinitely more tender. Without intending to, he gave me the opportunity to see that unconditional love still exists inside of me. And to truly be present, in each moment and with each breath. And for that, I am eternally grateful. Because I now know that I am ready to fall in love again. And after ninety-six months of dating, that is cause for one hell of a celebration.

GOOD-BYE LITTLE MISS PERFECT

When I was younger, I used to value perfection. I thought if I appeared perfect, life would be one big party. I thought if we all looked good and if we all appeared happy and functional, well, that's what it was all about. In addition to having inherited the dreaded "perfection" gene, I was raised in a family that generally seemed to value it, or something very close to it (especially one branch), and it was a lesson that I absorbed and held close to my heart.

It often felt more about appearance and what others thought of you and your life, not so much about what you were really feeling or what *you* thought about your life. You didn't express strong opinions, you didn't readily admit to mistakes, you didn't argue in public, you didn't question authority—and God forbid that you actually held a debate at the dinner table.

Conflict and nonconformity wasn't the way to fit in. Or to have people like you. Or to keep the boat from tipping over. And God knows, you didn't want anyone thinking your boat might be ready to sink. At least that was my takeaway.

No one was harder on me than myself. Many people know what this is like—holding yourself up to impossibly high standards. I have no doubt that my own parents were raised in much the same way, and like all of us, and were just doing what they knew best.

Even after I had children, I still wanted that illusion of perfection. The perfect marriage, the perfect husband, the perfect children, the perfect home. Or at least the striving for the perfect home, even in the midst of plaster dust and endless renovations.

But there are a number of blessings in death. There are a number of blessings in widowhood. And one of those blessings is that you stop trying to be perfect. You stop attempting to create an illusion. And it's not just that you stop—it's that you have no choice but to stop. At least I didn't. You don't have the energy to keep pretending. To keep putting up a front. To keep trying to be Little Miss Perfect.

Your husband is dead, and who really cares what anyone thinks of what you do or say. It's the same sort of liberation that I imagine comes with old age. You know how you always hear eighty-five-year-old women spouting inappropriate commentary and witty obscenities? Exactly!

It's pure freedom. Pure joy. Pure…perfection.

You suddenly are keenly aware of how short and how unpredictable life can be, and you're not going to sit around, following the rules or saving the good silver for special occasions, because you realize now it's all a bunch of ridiculousness. And what's on your mind is going to come spilling out.

Even if you're at a fancy restaurant. And everyone is listening. Besides, it would most likely be the highlight of their day.

NOT THE END

At this point, all of these potentially perfect endings qualify more as happy and fascinating surprises along the journey that is my life after death, rather than actual endings. Who really wants an *ending*, anyway? That means there's nothing left. Nada. No more bricks left to lay as you're building your path. And what fun would that be?

If you have an ending, then you may as well be...dead. And I've already had enough on that topic. So instead, here are a few updates.

Olivia is doing wonderfully *not* being at the college where her father and I met. And I'm doing wonderfully, as well. In fact, I've sometimes found myself feeling a bit guilty that I'm not missing her as much as I once imagined I would. I used to think I'd be sitting here, wallowing in sadness over her departure. But instead, I'm so busy with life that I've actually found myself appreciating the fact that I have our entire "girls' bathroom" all to myself. I can find my eye makeup remover again, and my hairbrush doesn't go missing! College has its perks. I'm wondering why I ever thought I'd find this transition so difficult, and I'm wondering who these women are who require years of therapy to recover from their children fleeing the nest.

I'm loving my new relationship with my fabulous, witty, creative daughter. She's not a child anymore, and I'm appreciating her in an entirely new way.

The coma guy is much better off without me and will surely meet someone who will be awed by his every breath, his every thoughtful word, and who will be capable of loving him exactly as he is. And isn't that what we all deserve?

And the guy with the fabulously perfect hair? He may not be boy-friend material, but he can count me in as a friend and can keep sharing his wondrous words with me for as long as he wants to (even if his big dog does occasionally eat my entire $5.75 bag of organic granola). Because his real-life words have been, at times, better than even the best sex I've ever had. And definitely better than text messages from men who have little to offer other than fancy dinners and lingering divorce drama. And one day far, far in the future, when I'm in one of my self-designed Girl Scout Dropout retirement homes, reminiscing about all of the scintil-lating adventures I had during my widowhood, he might still be able to snag a woman who would actually enjoy peeing in an outhouse. And I might actually be genuinely happy for him.

I've realized I don't need a happily-ever-after and I don't need to find the perfect man to make my "weak chapter" a bit stronger. My life, even without the proverbial Prince Charming (*gasp!*), has become its own perfect ending. And I'm both shocked by that and more than just a teensy bit thrilled. Because once you realize you don't need something, you usually graciously receive it. And it's usually not in the specific FedEx box in which you imagined it would arrive. So, even though I now know with ab-solute certainty that I don't need Mr. Right, I know with even greater certainty that he is out there somewhere, galloping to-wards me. And believe me, I'm ready for him.

Recently, I had the thrill of speaking at the launch party for my Girl Scout Dropout venture, a project I've envisioned for as long as I can remember. And it's not just a vision anymore. It's real. I proudly sported my long-awaited "More Support Than an Underwire Bra" badge—a round green treasure, à la scouting badges, featuring a decidedly non-scouting-like sexy black bra. It's a symbol of women sharing strength and laughter in the face of life's challenges, both large and small. It's a symbol of camaraderie, support, and a collective *I'm living life on my terms* attitude.

It's also a very personal symbol of my own struggles, dreams, visions, and humor in the face of tragedy. The day I picked up those badges from our vendor here in Portland, I called my good friend and marketing guru from my car, and the happiness of a woman who had dropped out of Girl Scouts thirty-nine years earlier emanated from each cell of my body as I proclaimed, "I have a box of bra badges in my back seat. I can die now, with no regrets."

The best part is, I meant it.

Today, I mailed out a number of booklets containing my Irreverent Widow stories to widows who've reached out to me. And I was happily able do it without asking them for their credit card numbers, because of my Irreverent Widow Fund—which I created due to my steadfast and unwavering belief that you shouldn't have to pay to grieve.

My dreams are all becoming a reality, and meanwhile, I'm watching my wonderful and magical children, now nineteen, sixteen, and thirteen, turn into wonderful and magical human beings with their own talents, their own beliefs, and their own agendas.

Olivia, as we've seen, is thriving. Holden is now taller than me, terrorizing me with his new driving skills, and still amazes and humbles me on a daily basis with his kind heart and wonderfully hilarious old-soul take on life—the perfectly rare blend of Zen and sarcasm. Meanwhile, Cole continues to delight me with his incredibly refined sense of humor, his boundless energy and determination, and his newfound love of acting. His ability to don a costume and deliver lines in front of an audience full of strangers—and harder still family members—floors me.

And although I will always in my heart of hearts wish Drew were walking beside me, holding my hand, I can't help but feel I was destined for this. However much I wish he were here to celebrate my accomplishments with me, and to see how wonderfully our children are turning out, I fully realize that were he here, I'd not have accomplished these things. I wouldn't be on this road.

So onward I go. With a smile in my heart for the love I know I've been fortunate to have had, and for that which I know is yet to come.

And I thank Gandhi, Drew, and my God-given sense of humor for preventing me from committing suicide in those bleakest days of widowhood. I've laughed until I've cried, and cried until I laughed. And I'm going to keep laughing as much as possible, because it may not be as easy to laugh when you're dead.

FINIS

POSTSCRIPT

And just when you thought you'd heard the last of me…

As you might imagine, selecting photographs for this book was not the most joyous part of my journey into author-dom. I had a closet full of boxes containing thousands of photos documenting my entire love affair and life with Drew and our children, and they were all precious to me. In tears during much of the photo selection process, I kept a wad of Kleenex stuffed into my left palm as I shuffled through stacks of printed memories with my right.

I'd warned my children in advance about the photo phase, and although they understood, they looked at me as if to say, *Just please move on to book number two, because we cannot tolerate much more of your weepiness.*

Truth be told, I'd dreaded this final part of the book-birthing process, and had avoided it for as long as humanly possible. Being a natural born procrastinator with ADD tendencies, it was easy to find a million things to do other than what I knew needed to be done.

Select book photos was right up there with *Clean the toilets.*

Early on in the book development process, my editor had generously offered to assist in the selection of the final images once I got to that stage. And so here I was, a year-and-a-half later, emailing him my top fifty. Of course, as always, I had the final say—but I was both relieved and thankful to have had his help in whittling it down to a mere twenty.

I was quite happy with all of the chosen photos. Well, all but one—the one of Drew and me during our first summer of being *in love*, the summer between our junior and senior years of college. The summer of 1982.

There had undoubtedly been more than one copy of that romantic college photo, and the small, cropped version I had tucked away in a tiny album that resided in the top drawer of my lingerie bureau was scanned and slated for the book— yet as I prepared to send the final images off to my designer, a wash of melancholy came over me: I could still envision the uncropped version, and I so wished I could have used it, instead.

Where the hell was the original?

I knew it must be somewhere, and that perhaps it was even still in my possession, but the thought of digging back into the archives of my linen closet was too depressing. I finally went to sleep, having decided that I'd just have to be happy with what I had, rather than torment myself further.

The next day, one of my children brought in the mail and handed me two envelopes. One was from my daughter's college and appeared to contain the patiently awaited financial aid information for her upcoming fall semester. I feared this letter more than I welcomed it, since Prince Charming hadn't yet shown up with an offer to subsidize her tuition payments, and a change for the worse in financial aid offerings wouldn't bode well for our family budget.

The other envelope had the return address of one of Drew's nephews, his sister's son, Nicholas. Now, although I love Nicholas and see him once a year at the family Christmas Eve gathering, we are not pen pals. In fact, I'm quite certain that the only communiqués I've ever received from him via snail mail have been a wedding invitation and two baby announcements.

So I was a bit perplexed by this oddly lumpy envelope with his address in the upper left corner.

Curious—and not in the correct frame of mind to open the college envelope—I opened the lumpy envelope first.

As I flattened the folded edge of the sheet of paper that popped out from beneath the flap, I think I stopped breathing for a second. There it was: the photograph. The 1982-first-summer-we-were-in-love photograph. Five inches by seven inches of pure, uncropped miracle.

As my eyes filled with tears (preceding a full-blown waterfall), I read the following words:

Dear Sandi,

How are you? I was putting a small nightstand in a bedroom of ours the other day, and this letter and picture fell from underneath the drawer. I had the nightstand for many years and it must have come from my grandmother's house when she was moved to the nursing home. I hope all is well with you and the kids.

Sincerely,

Nicholas

I immediately knew that nightstand—it was Drew's. A piece of colonial antiquity with a single drawer. "Grandmother's house" was, of course, the house Drew had grown up in. His mother had died years ago, and the contents of her home had been sprinkled around to different family members even before her passing. So this nightstand had been around the block a few times. And moved more than a few times. And still…these treasures had somehow remained safely hidden…wedged behind the drawer of the small bedside table.

The letter he referred to was five pages long—written on yellowed, five-by-seven sheets of paper. The peacock blue printing at the top of each page said "EJP, Inc. Water, Waste Water and Drainage Materials." Drew's family had a construction business, and he'd worked there during his college summers. This was no doubt a free advertising notepad from a company they did business with, and had come from his father's office.

Highly romantic. And all too perfect. It was Drew to a T, and it made me laugh out loud. Had it been written on Crane's 100 percent linen notepaper with his engraved initials at the top, I would have suspected a forgery. His uncanny (and unintentional) ability to express genuine romance via items not innately romantic was one of the things I loved most about him.

Although I have reams of paper in the form of love letters from my late husband, this was different. It was written in a rather poetic, abbreviated style, and as I read through it (and through my tears) I slowly realized it was a foreshadowing of what would eventually be our life story.

It began with "I look into soft clear spheres of hazy crystal blue, and see a future of dreams with you," and ended with "they are lovers, they are friends, and they are forever."

It was filled with symbolism and meaning…a description of me in a pure white dress and him in black…of sparkling fireflies floating up to the heavens and turning into constellations…of his seeing the anxious child inside of me and wanting to love me and guard me as I slept…of him looking into my eyes for strength, and of my love filling him with magic.

Reading it, I was reminded of how he did soothe that hurt child inside of me, how he was the consistent and unconditionally loving man I'd never had in my life growing up, and how, when he was ill, he did indeed look to me to provide the strength that sustained him.

As you might imagine, I wept uncontrollably for a good long time while reading this letter of love from thirty years ago. They were tears of happiness. Tears of thanks. Tears of knowing that the gift that had arrived so unexpectedly (and with such profoundly perfect timing) in an envelope from Massachusetts was a sign that Drew is still with me, still present. And that somehow, no matter how meaningless and unfair and random we might sometimes feel life can be…it's not.

Because if I never believed in a higher order or a higher energy and power at work in the universe, this convinced me.

I felt as if Drew had given me one last tender and passionate kiss…the final on top of the millions we'd shared since our first one, thirty-three years earlier.

And, somehow…it doesn't surprise me in the least. It's just the kind of romantic thing he would have done. Even in the afterlife.

So, thank you, my love, for sending me on my way with your final message.

And thank you, Nicholas, for being the messenger.

CPSIA information can be obtained at www.ICGtesting.com
Printed in the USA
BVOW022233221112

306157BV00005B/2/P